The Longest Mile

Nine Days in the Great Smoky Mountains

Ryan Watkins

Printed in the United States of America

First Printing, 2016

Credits
Cover Illustration: Jeremy Jones
Copy Editor: Lisa Gatzen
Author Photo: Bo Shell

ISBN-13: 978-1533374059
ISBN-10: 1533374058

Ryan Watkins
1512 Chattahoochee Circle
Roswell, GA 30075

www.mryanwatkins.com

Days

Day Zero

Standing Bear Farms

"DO YOU GUYS PARTY?" Mike the shuttle driver asked in a distinctly grizzled, southern accent.

Though we had only been in the shuttle for twenty minutes or so, this was the first indication of the adventure that awaited us. Mike must have known that we were a motley bunch just by looking at us. It took him a few minutes to get comfortable before he asked, but he asked nonetheless.

"That depends on what you mean by party," Jeremy responded from the back seat of the old pickup truck.

I had known Jeremy for just over a year through working together at a cell phone insurance company, where we had quickly bonded over our love of the outdoors, delicious lunches and questionably immature senses of humor. As long as I had known him, Jeremy had made no secret about his partying past, but at forty, he had since calmed down and become a respectable member of corporate America. Standing just over six feet tall, thin and dark with a haircut that would have made Morrissey proud, despite the tattoos and general bad boy persona, Jeremy was far away from his rebellious youth and the troubles that often brings.

"Y'all smoke?" Mike offered without hesitation.

"Absolutely," I told him excitedly.

"Here man, pack this," he said, handing me a small metal tin. I opened it to find a glass one-hitter and a small baggie of pot. I was sitting in the front of the truck, riding passenger alongside Mike.

I packed the pipe and handed it to Mike. He puffed and passed it back to me. I took a hit. I then handed it to Chris in the back, who also wanted a puff.

Chris was Jeremy's younger brother and the third member of our group. At thirty-two, he was my age, a little heavier than Jeremy, but not by much, and stood about as tall as his brother. He was a ginger through and through and had a patchy beard when we departed Jeremy's home in Atlanta. I had first met him that day, but for weeks leading up to the hike, Jeremy had promised that Chris and I would hit it off and quickly become buddies. It hadn't taken long to mesh with Chris. The drive from Atlanta to the Great Smoky Mountains National Park was filled with witty banter and much laughter. He had a library of amazing experiences in his life, including a summer spent camping in Alaska, a snowboarding hobby that had taken him around the world, a catalog of hiking trips that would have made a National Geographic photographer proud and, I suspect, many more adventures that he probably never shared.

Jeremy and Chris had both been born in North Georgia and were shaped early by their involvement with the Jehovah's Witness faith. Jeremy had once told me that their mother had strictly adhered to the faith's teachings, but he and his brother rebelled in their own ways early in life.

Chris puffed on the one-hitter and passed it back to me. I packed it again, took a puff and handed it back to Mike.

The three of us had ridden up to Fontana Dam earlier that day to meet our shuttle, which would take us from the south end of the Great Smoky Mountains National Park to Standing Bear Farms, a hostel a few miles north of the park entrance. Mike, our driver, was the hostel owner's brother and more than happy to make sure we had a good time during the ride.

On the drive to Standing Bear, we talked gear.

My pack was a nearly ten-year-old Osprey and included my hammock setup (hammock, straps, my rainfly, rope, hardware, sleeping pad and bug net), two sleeping bags, a sleeping bag liner, clothes, flip flops, cigarettes, my cook kit (a small wood-burning stove and pot), toiletries, rope, clothes, electronics and battery chargers, a host of small trinkets, a waterproof pack cover, a trash compactor bag for interior protection, water filtration, plastic water bottles, and, of course, my food and water.

In total, my pack weighed somewhere around fifty pounds with the food and water included, close to the maximum manufacturer recommended weight the pack should support and even closer to the maximum recommended weight my body could carry mile after mile. I also brought along two lightweight aluminum trekking poles that I had purchased a few months ahead of the hike.

I had spent several hours each night in the weeks leading up to the trip packing, repacking and optimizing the space inside my backpack. As we moved closer to the actual date, I found myself adding more and subtracting less. On the last night before our hike, a Saturday, I was finally able to finagle all of the gear into the perfect spots to fit everything. Barely. My Atmos bulged at the seams.

For months, Jeremy and I had made weekly trips to REI and other outfitter stores in the Atlanta area near our work to gather supplies.

I watched countless YouTube videos of hiker experiences from around the world and made every effort to immerse myself in backpacking culture leading up to the adventure. I read reviews on which dehydrated meals tasted the best, which boots offered the most comfort for long distance hiking, how to properly strap a fifty-pound pack to your back and dozens of other related topics in an attempt to prepare myself.

Chris was from Pensacola, Florida and prepared himself with a single shopping spree on Amazon a few weeks ahead of the trip. As careful as Jeremy and I had been with our purchases and research, Chris based his gear choices on online customer reviews and the expediency of shipping.

The heaviest burden I carried was my food. In total, I had around twenty pounds of consumables in my pack, separated into two eight liter waterproof stuff sacks. While selecting and packing the food, I was convinced I had not brought enough to sustain myself over the one hundred-something miles we had originally planned to hike. My biggest concern was not my fitness or the quality of my gear. My biggest concern was whether or not I would be hungry at the end of each day.

My estimated daily caloric intake was somewhere around two thousand calories. But when the trail demands five or six thousand calories a day, eating the daily recommended allotment of food is simply not enough to stave off hunger. I was excited at the prospect of losing a little bit of weight on the trip, though. I had told Jeremy at work the week before we left that I was going to lose ten pounds.

I packed nine days' worth of food into nine individual one-gallon Ziploc bags. Inside were meat sticks, jerky, candy bars, mixed nuts, tortillas, peanut butter, dehydrated meals, breakfast bars, energy bars and instant iced coffee. Even with all of that food, I was convinced I would be starving throughout each day.

Many hikers, especially those who are attempting the entire Appalachian Trail, quickly learn how to cut weight from their packs. It's not uncommon for a hiker to begin the trail with a pack as heavy, or even heavier, than the one I brought into the park. Food choice becomes as critical as any piece of gear that a hiker may carry, as weight and caloric count vastly outweigh the importance of taste.

I knew that weight would be an issue because of our scheduling and having to carry eight days of food from the onset, but as I prepared for the trip by carrying my pack around my apartment for hours at a time, I began to realize how much of a burden I actually had strapped to my back. It would be several days and quite a bit of food consumed before the pack was a comfortable weight.

I knew I would need everything (and more) that I had stuffed inside my pack. In the weeks before the hike, I had carefully read through dozens of online articles and watched as many gear videos as I could to get a sense of what it was that I would actually need on the trail. I even had a plan for how to best deal with my trash.

We had no stops planned anywhere close to actual civilization during our eight days in the woods and whatever we brought in with us, save the trash, would have to stay with us throughout the entire trip. There were two tourist areas near non-hikers, one at Newfound Gap, basically in the middle of the park along US Route 441, and the other at Clingman's Dome, the highest point in the park and on the Appalachian Trail, where we could ditch our wrappers, cigarette butts and used packaging.

Before we began, I emailed the information address at Great Smoky Mountain National Park to ask about possible mail drops where I could send myself supplies, like food, to pick up when I arrived. The ranger who responded was sympathetic but had no good news to offer. There were no places to send or receive mail drops. Even in the world of modern conveniences and instant gratification, there are still places that are as close to wild and free as possible. The Smokies, thanks to its vast remoteness, is still one of those places.

***

The Appalachian Mountains formed some two hundred million years ago when the world looked very different. The common scientific theory states the North American and African tectonic plates smashed together and pushed the land upward, forming some of the world's oldest mountains sometime during the formation and breakup of the Pangea supercontinent.

Millions of years ago, the mountains themselves were much taller, perhaps as tall as today's European Alps or North American Rocky Mountains. Time had eroded away much of the mountains' height, and today the Appalachians are only a distant memory of their former glory. Regardless of how great they may have once been, the mountains in the Great Smoky Mountains National Park remain a formidable challenge for hikers, especially those who enter the park unprepared. More than thirty miles of the seventy-one mile stretch of Appalachian Trail through the Great Smoky Mountain National Park is over five thousand feet in elevation, making it the highest bit of hiking thru-hikers attempt each year.

The park was dedicated by President Franklin D. Roosevelt in 1940 and today consists of more than half a million square acres of protected forests, flora, rivers, waterfalls, mountains and wildlife. It was unique in its formation, as large parks at the time were typically privately funded. The U.S. government, however, began to see the wisdom of preserving natural spaces in the early part of the 20th century and took this preservation seriously, helping to financially back the park.

"The old frontier, that put the hard fibre in the American spirit and the long muscles on the American back, lives and will live in these untamed mountains to give to the future generations a sense of the land from which their forefathers hewed their homes," Roosevelt said during his dedication speech at Newfound Gap on September 2, 1940. More than seventy-five years later, Roosevelt's words would still ring true.

Though the park received federal money, a hefty chunk of the funding came privately from John D. Rockefeller, Jr., son of Standard Oil founder John D. Rockefeller. If naturalist Benton MacKaye is the father of the Appalachian Trail, the junior Rockefeller would undoubtedly be the father of the Great Smoky Mountains National Park and many other national parks that millions of Americans continue to enjoy long after his passing.

"Think of giving not as a duty but as a privilege," Rockefeller, Jr. once famously said. A monument to Rockefeller still stands at Newfound Gap as a testament to his generous donation and sense of wild adventure.

***

"You boys are gonna have a great time," Mike said in his stoned stupor as we cruised up the interstate. He had become excitable after smoking and would speed up slightly or coast slowly depending on whether or not he was talking.

He talked about his experiences in the park with his wife. He told us about the hostel where we were staying. He pointed out sights and landmarks along the way. He talked about his Honda CRV and how it was the best car that he'd ever owned. He told us how much he hated the truck he was now driving. Mike liked to talk.

Later in the ride, the conversation turned to music.

"I'm really into metal," Mike told us. "I love it when people combine different styles of music, like metal and bluegrass or metal and rap. Y'all ever hear about that?"

"Oh, yeah," Chris responded.

"Have you guys ever heard of the Insane Clown Posse?" Mike asked somewhat timidly. "I'm no Faygo drinking Juggalo, but man, I love the Insane Clown Posse!"

"I'm not sure I've ever really listened to them," I told him. "I've only heard a couple of their songs." The three of us withheld our collective urges to laugh.

"You really should give it a listen, man. You'd love it!"

"Yeah, sure," Jeremy responded. "I think the fact that you said you're not a Juggalo means you're definitely a Juggalo!"

Eventually, Mike moved on to politics, discussing current world events with a surprisingly liberal overtone and exclaiming the brilliance of Massachusetts Senator Elizabeth Warren.

At first glance, it would have been easy to assume Mike was just another backwoods hillbilly from western North Carolina who loved his guns and his God. He was not. Mike was a pot smoking, ponytail-sporting, liberal voter from the Tar Heel State. The man confused the hell out of me.

8

The shuttle ride took about two hours from Fontana Dam, our eventual end point, to Standing Bear Farms Hostel, just north of Great Smoky Mountain National Park and a favorite resting destination among the annual northbound thru-hikers attempting the entire twenty-one hundred-something mile Appalachian Trail.

Midway through the shuttle ride, the realization of the immense distance we had committed ourselves began to set in. All three of us began questioning our desire to actually backpack the entire park's length. Still, we were confident. The mountains had not yet tested us, and we had yet to find a valid reason to doubt our collective ability. After what seemed like an eternity in the truck, we arrived at Standing Bear Farms in mid-afternoon.

It's not uncommon for hikers coming north on the trail to take a zero day at Standing Bear before tackling the Cherokee National Forest, another intensely difficult section of the Appalachian Trail further north of the Smokies.

A zero-day is a day of rest for hikers where they walk on the trail as little as possible. Hikers take zero or near zero days as often as necessary. Injuries, fatigue or the need to resupply are common reasons hikers leave the trail for short periods.

Just a few days up the trail from Standing Bear sat Hot Springs, another favorite spot for thru-hikers looking for rest and relaxation. Some hikers have been known to skip Standing Bear in favor of Hot Springs. Others have little choice and are forced to rest or resupply at the first opportunity they come across.

Standing Bear Farms was a quaint hostel located just a few hundred yards off the trail north of the park. The compound had a shared bunk space, with ten-or-so beds, a private cabin and an even more secluded single-person tree house. The common areas included a clothes washing station, a small library, a fire ring, a surprisingly well-stocked commissary and a little stream that ran through the center of the property. The hostel buildings could comfortably sleep somewhere around twenty hikers, though there was a field for tent campers, as well. Jeremy and Chris decided to spend the first night in the tents, while I opted to sleep in my hammock. This would be the first time I had actually slept outside in a hammock overnight. I was excited about the new experience.

As we pulled into Standing Bear Farms, Mike ushered us to the facility administrator where we received a crash course in hostel etiquette. Staying on the property was $15 per night, not unreasonable, but for tent camping, I had assumed it would have been a little cheaper. The bunks were full when we arrived in the early evening, and there were already a few hikers setting up tents before sundown. Most of the hikers walking around had arrived earlier in the day and were planning to sleep overnight before continuing north.

The hostel offered amenities that hikers rarely find outside of cities and towns along the trail. WIFI, a washing machine, dryer, reading material and civilized pleasures awaited hikers there. Standing Bear Farms was also a common mail-drop destination where hikers or their families would mail supplies to themselves like food and replacement gear. We took advantage of the amenities, most notably the commissary.

Shortly after arriving, we ran into a thru-hiker who commented on our obviously green appearance. While Jeremy and Chris scouted the tent sites for a suitable spot, I went in search for trees that could accommodate my hammock.

"You boys must be just starting," the hiker said as the three of us walked toward the tent sites. "You look clean!"

We explained our plans, but the hiker seemed too tired to be impressed with our preparation or end goal. He had just finished the section we were attempting in reverse and was more interested in eating and finding a good night's sleep than hearing anyone's stories.

After Jeremy and Chris had set up their tents and I had put together my hammock rig on the other side of the bunk house, we gathered around the fire ring to talk about the upcoming challenge with a few hikers who had just made it through the park. A couple of older thru-hikers were more than willing to share their experiences with us while they ate.

"What was the weather like in the park?" I asked the group of three or four thru-hikers.

They all laughed at the question.

"It depends on the day," one of the hikers responded through a chuckle.

"Rain. Lots of rain," another said.

"It's supposed to be cold later this week," the third chimed in. "Maybe even snow!"

Snow? In May? That was ridiculous. The thought seemed absurd. It was a comfortable sixty-five degrees at Standing Bear Farms that evening and even warmer back home in Atlanta.

The weather in the Smokies has always been notoriously unpredictable. The reports for the week showed a mix of rain, cold temperatures and a few sunny, clear days toward the end of our planned hike. The coldest day on the charts was Thursday slated for thirty-one degrees, just below freezing. For early May, this seemed impossible to us. The difference in elevation from Atlanta, just over a thousand feet above sea level, to Clingman's Dome, the park's highest point at over 6,800 feet, meant that temperatures would be much colder than those we had recently left, but snow?

We had prepared as best we could leading up to the hike. I had several layers of clothing, a few different shirts and a jacket that should work to keep me warm during the evening in freezing temperatures. I even had a poncho with me in case the rain or cold wind decided to whip me. All of these items fit neatly into a small stuff sack in my pack.

The Smokies is also one of the wettest areas of the country. As much as eighty-five inches of rain dumps on the park annually with the largest concentration occurring during the spring months. We had expected rain later in the week, but tonight, we were more concerned with catching a buzz.

Once we learned that Standing Bear Farms offered beer, our already good moods lifted even higher. Beer and other alcohol are typically a luxury on the Appalachian Trail. Most thru-hikers simply don't drink booze unless they're off trail.

We bought a six-pack of Standing Bear's finest booze, classic American Budweiser, and laughed and drank until well after dark around the hostel's unused fire ring.

We talked about bears with the other hikers. All of the men we had met earlier had seen at least one during their five or six days in the park. One of the hikers showed us pictures on his phone from the previous day of a bear walking around just outside of a shelter. The prospect of seeing a bear in the wild was both thrilling and terrifying.

There are more than two bears per every square mile of land in the Smoky Mountains. Some estimates put as many as two thousand bears in and around the Smokies. And while attacks on humans are incredibly rare, bears have been known to steal a hiker's pack or bag looking for food. In truth, they are usually more of a nuisance than a physical threat, though no encounter with a wild animal is completely safe from danger. Especially when that wild animal is a hungry, four hundred pound beast accustomed to being at the top of its local food chain.

The warnings were clear. We were going to be as cautious as possible, not because we were fearful of an attack, but because if we lost any amount of food midway through the hike, there would be no real way to replace it without traveling to Gatlinburg to resupply. Depending on where that might happen during the trip, we could go several days without eating.

None of us had any real way to prevent an attack or deter a bear from coming at us other than our voices and whatever stones or rocks we could find on the trail immediately in front of us. Some hikers, especially solo hikers, will add small bells to the outside of their packs to make noise as they walk along the trail. This is supposed to warn any bears of a hiker's arrival and help facilitate a scampering escape. Other hikers would carry bear spray, a type of potent mace, that could, at least in theory, temporarily blind or hinder a bear long enough to allow a hiker to escape a potential attack.

"It would be a shame if we didn't see a bear," we said to one another at various points that evening.

Shortly after, another thru-hiker made himself two frozen pizzas. Each was for sale at a whopping $10 a pop, the most expensive food item available in the commissary. Nearly every other food item for sale in the commissary was reasonably priced, but the markup on pizza, a treat for tired and hungry hikers, was monstrous.

The thru-hiker stacked both pizzas on top of each other and chowed away. Jeremy, Chris and I made hot dogs and ate Pringles with a slight envy of the hiker's $20 double pizza dinner. I drank a Yoo-hoo.

The administrator of the hostel, on his way to refill a large propane tank sometime that evening, crashed the hostel's shuttle van into the small stream running through the property. Most of the hikers found this hilarious, especially when a tow truck had to be called later to rescue the stuck van.

Jeremy took photos of the old Dodge van as it teetered on the edge of the stream. We were certain that the impact had damaged the drive shaft since the van's bottom sat squarely on the rocky creek bank.

Several of the hikers gathered around the crash site to watch the tow truck pull the Dodge from the stream in the dark. We drank our last few beers, made jokes and laughed at the absurdity of the predicament. Even one of the hostel dogs got in on the comedy and sat in the driver's seat to pose for a photo for Jeremy.

"Well there goes our hostel fees," I said as the tow truck drove away. It couldn't have been cheap to have the van towed out of the creek. Much to our surprise, the resilient old van drove off without any noticeable problems.

After a while, the hostel administrator began to feel a little better after having the van yanked from the creek and brought out a jar of moonshine for anyone willing to try it. A few of the thru-hikers indulged themselves. Jeremy, Chris and I had a few sips each, as well.

The administrator was tall and had an impressive ponytail. He looked and sounded as high as a kite. It was no wonder he had backed the van into the stream.

Once our booze ran dry, the three of us were anxious for the next day to arrive. We wanted an early start as our plan was to hike up some eleven miles to Cosby Knob shelter, the second shelter inside the park for southbound hikers.

I set up my hammock next to a small creek between two pine trees under my rainfly and crawled inside. After a few moments of shifting around, I found the most comfortable position and readied myself for sleep.

That night as I drifted off, I imagined what was to come. I dreamed of mountains, hills, rivers, waterfalls and adventure.

Day One
The Last Mile is the Longest

A COMMON SAYING on the Appalachian Trail is "the first mile is the hardest; the last mile is the longest." This phrase was especially true as we set out on the first day of our section hike and experienced for ourselves a shock introduction to life on the world's most famous hiking trail.

Our plan was fairly simple, considering the distance we were to travel. We planned to hike just shy of one hundred miles over eight days, stopping at shelters along the Appalachian Trail heading south through the Great Smoky Mountains National Park. We would occasionally seek out other interesting spots along the way, diverting north or south off of the trail to visit several of the park's best-known natural landmarks.

Most hikers, and almost all thru-hikers, typically go from south to north along the Appalachian Trail, even those attempting a section hike like us. Our hope was that we would stay clear of any "hiker bubbles" and meet a new group of fresh and interesting people every night along the way. We had also been told that hiking the trail north to south was easier on the legs.

The start of the thru-hiking season typically begins in mid to late March every year at Springer Mountain in Georgia. Making it to the Smokies takes a few solid weeks of hiking, typically around twenty or more days for most thru-hikers. That meant that we would run into quite a few groups of hikers as we made our way through the mountains on our section hike the first week of May.

Thru-hikers have always tried to hike with the season, starting in the cold in Georgia and walking north with spring for as long as possible. Eventually, the summer heat will catch up to hikers, but it's possible to knock out a good chunk of the trail with decently moderate temperatures before the dog days of summer.

When discussing the trip with anyone who would listen in the months leading up to the hike, nearly everyone I talked to who knew anything about backpacking suggested that our group hike the Benton MacKaye Trail instead of the Appalachian Trail section through the Smokies. The reasoning here was that the Benton MacKaye Trail would offer the same type of hiking experience, but the crowds would be thinner throughout. Plus, in the span of a couple of trips, it would be possible to complete the entire Benton MacKaye Trail, where it could take a lifetime of section hiking to finish the entire Appalachian Trail, an unlikely prospect at this point in my life.

***

The Benton MacKaye Trail runs alongside the Appalachian Trail for about two hundred and ninety miles beginning in North Georgia near the start of the Appalachian Trail at Springer Mountain and ending at the northeast tip of the Great Smoky Mountains National Park at Davenport Gap. The terrain is very similar, though there seemed to be longer stretches of flatter portions in the Smokies on the Benton MacKaye Trail, especially closer to the end of the trail in the southern end near Fontana Lake where the trail hugged the lake's shoreline for many miles.

But, the Benton MacKaye Trail is not the Appalachian Trail. The allure of the Appalachian Trail simply doesn't compare to some of the lesser known trails in the country, despite namesakes and histories.

Benton MacKaye was instrumental in the formation of the Appalachian Trail and was an advocate for natural beauty and the outdoors during a time in American history of growing industrialization and technological advancement. Anyone who has hiked the Appalachian Trail has MacKaye and his conservation advocacy to thank for the experience.

"The Appalachian Trail is conceived as the backbone of a super reservation and primeval recreation ground covering the length (and width) of the Appalachian Range itself, its ultimate purpose being to extend acquaintance with the scenery and serve as a guide to the understanding of nature," MacKaye wrote on the conception of the Appalachian Trail.

We planned what we thought were moderate days, in terms of distance and difficulty, with our longest day ending up somewhere around fourteen miles. For someone who hikes several times a month, this seemed like a good balance between distance and the overall experience. I thought we would be inundated with waterfalls and mountaintop views. I thought we would be able to see everything the park had to offer in just a handful of days.

The Appalachian Trail runs just over seventy miles through the park, but many of the shelters and water sources were far enough off the trail that by the time a hiker has completed the Smokies, the total distance traveled is closer to eighty miles instead of the mapped seventy. We planned a few additional side hikes that would have added about twenty more miles to this total. It would be nearly impossible for us to calculate exactly how far we hiked during the trip, but we had a good sense of the estimated distance we planned.

***

After waking up in the morning, taking advantage of frozen Jimmy Dean sausage biscuits and Yoo-hoo from the commissary and packing up the gear, our group headed off into the park not entirely sure what to expect from the coming adventure.

We knew the hike would be difficult. We knew the mountains would throw every kind of imaginable weather and terrain at us before the end of the trip. We knew it was going to be cold. But, most importantly, we knew that we had a very long way to walk before we made it back to Fontana Dam.

It was our intention to weigh our packs at Standing Bear before we left. The running joke among our group ahead of the trip was how heavy our packs were, and we wanted to know who had the heaviest and bulkiest pack in the group. Unfortunately, we forgot to weigh the packs as we left the hostel and didn't realize until we were a little more than half a mile up the trail. By the time we remembered, it was too late to turn around and go back. As it turned out, winning the weight game was not as important as we initially made it out to be. In this case, it was better to not know. All three of us assumed we had the heaviest packs, and because each of us carried our own weight, all three of us were right in our own minds.

Jeremy, Chris and I had been planning a section hike of the seventy-one-mile section of the Appalachian Trail through the park that spans through two states, for nearly six months. The Great Smoky Mountains National Park is the country's most visited national park and for good reason. The mountains here are stunning, and the rolling clouds that cover many of the mountaintops that give the park its name are more often closer to a Tolkien-inspired fantasy world than our everyday reality. Millions of people would visit the park in any given year, and for good reason. It's gorgeous.

There is a majesty about the park and the mountains there not found in other places of the country or even other places in Appalachia. For our first trip together, we thought the Smokies was the perfect choice as it offered a demanding, but doable, challenge and was close to home.

Training for the hike meant doing what I already love: walking in the woods. Most weekends during the spring, summer and fall months, would find me hitting the trail with my daughter, walking along some river somewhere in North Georgia looking for waterfalls and other natural landmarks. In the last few years, my daughter Lucy and I had tackled some of Georgia's best trails: Duke's Creek, Raven Cliff, Panther Creek, Bear Creek and several others. None of those trails, however, had truly prepared me for what was to come in the Smokies.

Our group, excited by the prospect of actually beginning the adventure, made our way from the hostel south toward the park. We crossed into the park over the Pigeon River bridge after a bit of confusion with directions and made our way further south after walking under I-40. The river view here was a small sampling of what was to come, though we never made our way across a bridge this large or a river this wide again during the following days.

After a few miles of the trail, the pain of the elevation gain and total mileage for the day became apparent. Today was one of the longer days we had originally planned, some eleven miles and climbing nearly four thousand feet into the air. We walked along a pleasant, bubbling stream as we made our way upward. My legs began to tire from the constant incline. The stairs were brutal.

Jeremy had prepared for the hike by going to the gym and using a Stairmaster to train for the intense elevation gains. For weeks ahead of the trip, he was in the gym two or three times a week grinding out his legs, constantly climbing up the mechanical stairs, getting stronger.

I was not in the best shape, but my legs were one of the better parts of my physique. As often as I hiked leading up to the trip, and as often as I threw down ten mile days ahead of the hike, I thought nothing of the eleven miles planned for the opening day. I knew it would be difficult, but part of me assumed it would be the easy kind of difficult, where time was the most challenging aspect, not the actual activity itself.

It took only a few miles before the realization had come that the physical and mental challenges were very real. It seemed the park had a near-infinite number of mountains ahead of us, and I was simply not prepared for them. Step after step, the constant climb was exhausting.

As we worked our way up the trail early in the day, two thru-hikers came down the hill and told us they had seen a bear cub a mile or so back up the trail.

"We didn't see the mother, though," one of them told us.

"Be careful!" the other chimed in as they quickly made their way down the hill toward Standing Bear Farms.

We were vigilant, but nothing came that day.

A few grueling hours later, we came to Davenport Shelter, the last shelter in the park for the Appalachian Trail northbound thru-hikers and the first for southbound hikers, like us. A young couple was sitting just off the trail to the shelter enjoying an afternoon snack and rest. As we approached, they warned of bears and looked rather relieved to be leaving this portion of the trail.

"Is that the shelter down there?" I asked.

"Yeah," one of them responded. "It's a little off trail, but there are still some people there now."

We chatted briefly, mostly so I could catch my breath and prepare for the next bit of uphill. We parted ways shortly after. I benefitted from the brief break, but my energy quickly drained again.

We pushed on up the mountain. My pace began to slow until it became more of a crawl than a hike. Mile after mile, foot over foot, I began to feel the weight of my pack slowly drag me down. I was forced to stop several times and fell back further from the group until Chris and Jeremy were so far ahead of me that they couldn't be seen from the trail.

"Hike your own hike" is another common saying among hikers. My hike, unfortunately, was much slower than my compatriots, and they continued on ahead without me.

My shoulders ached. My hips, where the majority of the pack weight sat, ached. My calves and thighs ached. My entire body was slowly failing me with each step upward.

After a few more miles and what seemed like an eternity, I eventually caught up with Jeremy and Chris shortly after they had replenished their water supplies. We chatted briefly as they walked ahead of me on a switchback above. I told them to go ahead with their normal pace and that I would meet them at the shelter, Cosby Knob, later that afternoon. Looking at the time, it seemed completely reasonable to me that I would make it to the shelter before dark.

I was a few miles away from the shelter, but there was still plenty of sunlight left and the trail ahead looked as though it had finally reached the ridgeline. I was hopeful for some flat sections, or a little bit of downhill to help offset my slow speed. Those, unfortunately, never came.

My pace became my own as I settled in for a slow march up the mountain, now unconcerned with catching up to Jeremy and Chris. Several times I stopped on rock outcroppings or along the ridgeline to snap a poor quality photo of myself against the mountain-filled backdrop or to smoke a cigarette. It was a slow but beautiful hike under the newly green spring foliage. The temperature had steadily dropped all afternoon as the clouds began to collect in the distance.

The mountains in the valley below showed just how far I had climbed that day. It might not have seemed like a great distance at the time, but with the elevation and pack weight, the challenge was very real. I was still far from done, and I was not completely broken.

I sat on a small group of rocks overlooking the valley below and smoked a cigarette while enjoying the view. A northbound thru-hiker passed by and sat with me for a moment. We discussed the trail ahead and all of the sights he had seen during his short time in the park. By this point in the trail for northbound thru-hikers, more than two hundred and forty miles separated them from the traditional starting point at Springer Mountain in North Georgia. By comparison, I was barely eight miles into the trail and already my legs and lungs burned with exhaustion. Interestingly enough, I was about ten percent through my hike of the park. The northbound thru-hikers at the tail end of the park were also about ten percent through their hikes of the entire trail.

When I set off, I again wondered if I had made a mistake by agreeing to such a strenuous endeavor. I questioned my commitment, endurance and drive.

The clouds began to slowly roll over the mountains as I continued to fall farther beyond Jeremy and Chris. The Smokies are a remarkable place with unpredictable weather and constantly changing conditions. One moment was dry and sunny, the next a torrent of rain and wind thrashed unprepared hikers. This was part of the appeal for section hikers here. The thru-hikers I met, especially toward the end of their hikes through the Smokies, were more than happy to be leaving the park. Several hikers mentioned that this was the most difficult section of the hike they had encountered so far. Elevation here is a killer, but it doesn't get any better as you progress farther north until Virginia, most hikers told us, thanks to the weather and elevation.

The clouds continued to roll over the hills until the sky had turned from a pale blue to dark gray.

By late afternoon the rain came in full force. I was as prepared as I could be with a heavy poncho, a wide boonie hat, a waterproof cover for my pack and boots as waterproof as they could be. As darkness crept over the mountaintops, I began to worry that my leisurely pace in the afternoon had come back to bite me.

A short while later, the sun completely faded over the horizon and darkness enveloped the mountains above and valleys below.

Hiking at night was perilously difficult. Hiking in the darkness through the rain was even worse. The rocks became slippery and the discount Wal-Mart headlamp I had purchased ahead of the trip began to flicker on and off.

I checked my phone several times for my GPS location, but I wanted to save battery. It didn't matter, though. When I walked a tenth of a mile per hour, it would take me ten hours to walk a mile. That's the sad reality of hiking. I knew this, but the weather and constant uphill forced me to slug along at a slow and uneasy pace. I was amazed that my phone still had a signal. I was even more amazed that the water running down my arms and onto my clothes had not completely ruined any and everything in my shirt or pants pockets.

The rain quickly morphed into a full thunderstorm. It was the lightning that worried me the most. For the first time since childhood, I counted the seconds between every flash of light and every blast of deafening thunder. Hiking up the ridge, sometimes completely out of tree cover, meant that I was uncomfortably exposed to direct lightning only a mile or two away from me. I've never been scared of lightning. In fact, part of me has always found the flashes and booms fascinating, but out in the woods, in the darkness, the primal fear kicked in and my survival instincts prevented any enjoyment of the experience. Walking with two aluminum hiking poles did little to ease my insecurity, as well.

Flash.

One... Two... Boom!

Flash.

One... Boom!

The flashes of lightning bounced from raindrop to raindrop on the ridgeline all around me.

Any time the lightning was two or fewer miles from where I was hiking, I stopped and looked for cover. Hiding under a tree on a mountaintop during a lightning storm was probably not the best idea, but I had nowhere else to go. My only choice was to wait out the lightning and proceed when I felt safe.

I sat for nearly thirty minutes under a tree as lightning flashed all around me. The hills lit up with every strike. The clouds rolled over the ridgeline.

Eventually, I gave up attempting to push through and attempted to smoke a cigarette while waiting out the storm. A cold chill came over my body, and I began to shiver. Hiking in the cold was difficult, but the constant movement keeps the body warm and limber. Huddled under a tree trying to stay warm and dry was not easy, but I was convinced that dying by lightning would have been much worse.

I pictured my friends, hiking back down the trail in the morning, looking for my soaked, charred and electrocuted body. I began to resent them for continuing on without me, despite my insistence they do so. I had assured Jeremy and Chris that I would be okay and be just a little while behind them, but I seriously regretted the decision after spending too much time huddled under a tree, waiting out the thunderstorm. Part of me expected to see Jeremy and Chris hiking back down the trail looking for me.

My clothing was soaked through, and my poncho, despite being perfectly waterproof, didn't quite cover my entire body, especially my arms. Cold water seeped through my pants and down my arms as I waited for a break in the storm. It became darker and darker as my headlamp slowly drained away.

I was tired and began debating whether or not I should just set up camp along the shelter or if I should push on. Camping along the trail in the park was against regulations and carried with it a hefty $600 fine if caught. Still, the cost of the ticket would have been worth the price, if it meant I wouldn't drown or die from hypothermia. I assumed the rangers would understand that it was a life or death decision. I also assumed I would be ticketed regardless.

Eventually, the storm subsided enough for me to press on, and I came across a sign a short while later, a glorious, marvelous, gift from God. A sign! Cosby Knob was only 0.8 miles away.

I was ecstatic. After several hours of pushing through the paranoia-filled darkness convinced every drop of water behind me was a pair of eyes stalking me, I finally had a clear indication that I was headed in the right direction.

I continued on through the pouring rain. The lightning eased as the thunderstorm rolled down the mountains away from me, but there was no break in the rain.

The last mile was the longest. It was true that day and every day after.

Another hour or more hiking up the last mountain to reach Cosby Knob in the pouring rain was the most difficult experience of my life. Soaking wet, convinced I had mild hypothermia, I began to scream and shout into the night but was drowned out by the torrential downpour. Still, the release of anger and frustration felt good. What else could I do but walk and scream into the night?

"Where the fuck is the god damn shelter!?" I yelled. "FUCK!"

I walked on, shouting into the darkness at nothing in particular.

My headlamp finally succumbed to the wet and flickered its last flash. The rain had beaten that into submission, too.

I was convinced that I had walked well over the 0.8-mile mark and somehow missed the shelter, but I kept going in near total darkness. I would just keep walking until I found a shelter, any shelter, or I would die trying.

Shortly after I came to another sign pointing in the direction of Cosby Knob and nearly collapsed in exhaustion. I walked down the hill and under the cover of the roof before stripping off all my clothes and unpacking all of my gear onto the wooden bench outside of the shelter area. I had no idea what time it was, and I didn't care. I had somehow made it.

The contents of my pack exploded on the wooden bench as I pulled everything out. I did my best to hang my wet clothes, but unless I could magically find an electric clothes dryer in the back of the shelter, they would not dry that night.

I pulled out my sleeping bag and pad, hung my food on the steel bear cables just down the hill from the shelter and crawled onto the top bunk where I fell asleep wearing only thermal underwear. I slept as though I had found my deathbed.

The longest day of my life was finally over, and I had survived.

Day Two
Surviving Bear Attack

IN THE MORNING, I was one of the last to get out of my sleeping bag. Unsure of how long I had actually slept the night before, I was groggy and already exhausted before I had even begun the day. Down the hill from the shelter, I saw Jeremy packing up his tent and pack. Chris was below me in the shelter, waking up as well.

During the night, my neighbor had taken offense to my snoring and woke me up several times by touching my shoulders. As uncomfortable as I was by a stranger touching me in my sleep, I had no sympathy for his troubled night. Did he not know that I barely survived the previous day?

Luckily for him, my exhaustion prevented any meaningful overnight confrontations, though I did make a point to grumble each time he woke me.

"You made it!" Chris said with some relieved excitement when I finally began to stir.

"Barely," I responded.

"What time did you make it in?"

"I'm not sure. It could have been after midnight. Maybe even later. Probably later."

It was all a blur to me. My body ached, and I was still shivering from the night before. As I changed into dry clothes and ate breakfast, Jeremy came up to the shelter to eat, as well.

"I felt really bad about leaving you," he told me as he approached.

I was plainly disgruntled at the thought of the previous night's hike, but simply making it to the shelter the night before washed away much of my ill feelings toward my partners. I later found out that Jeremy had asked the thru-hikers in the shelter to make room for me because he knew I would be coming in much too late to set up any kind of sleeping arrangement. The thought of setting up a hammock in the darkness under a blanket of pouring rain was dreadful. This gesture won him some much-needed brownie points.

The three of us talked about the day ahead and the disaster that was the previous day's climb. The promise of adventure was ahead, and I began to feel better knowing that I had reconnected with the group.

Our original plan was to push past the next shelter, Tricorner Knob, all the way to Pecks Corner shelter. That total distance, somewhere around twelve and a half miles, was simply too much for us to tackle on the second day if we wanted to arrive before sunset. We decided to fall behind our planned schedule and stay at Tricorner Knob shelter that night instead. The revised distance was just shy of eight miles, and it was another long haul elevation gain, some seventeen hundred more feet up, we guessed. After our second day, the map showed a more balanced up and down ridge-walk until the last few days. There would be more than enough uphill to constantly challenge us, but at least the respite of downhill would eventually follow.

Getting behind schedule on just the second day was not good, but pushing the twelve miles to Pecks Corner meant another extremely late shelter arrival, something I could not do two nights in a row. We needed to lighten the burden and not hike through the dark. I needed a proper night's rest.

By the end of the second day on the trail, we were expecting to be right around six thousand feet above sea level and nearly twenty miles into the park. Tricorner Knob was one of the highest shelters in the park by elevation, and we were looking forward to the shorter day instead of the constant stairs up the mountains.

Despite the difficult day ahead of us, all three of us knew the hardest individual section of the entire trip, the hike to Cosby Knob from Standing Bear the day before, was behind us. This and the shortened distance of our revised itinerary gave us the slight morale boost we desperately needed as we set off for the day. Jeremy and Chris had both arrived at the shelter the night before in the darkness, as well, and both were also leaving difficult days behind.

About a quarter of a mile up the trail from the shelter, the aches and pains quickly returned. It was only the beginning of the day, but I was already suffering under the weight of the pack. I adjusted and readjusted my straps. I made every effort before setting off to find the perfect balance between hip and shoulder weight distribution. No matter how I situated the pack on my body, something somewhere would hurt.

I began to wonder if I was even going to make it through to the end, a scary thought just eleven miles into the trip. If the entire trail consisted of nonstop elevation gain and stair after fucking stair, there was no way I would make it to the end.

There was little time to question the options, and absolutely nothing that could be done at this point, besides hiking back down the mountain to Standing Bear Farms and spending the next eight days sleeping on a bunk, at $15 dollars a night, until the others arrived. That was not the experience I wanted from the Smokies.

We continued up the hills and unlike the previous day, there were actually a few flat and short downhill sections on the march to Tricorner Shelter. Despite those breaks, the vast majority of the hike continued the previous day's theme. We hiked ever higher and higher, though we were appreciative of the small moments of flat the mountains sometimes offered.

I attempted to lighten the mood several times that morning by retelling some of my favorite jokes, but they were largely received with awkward silence. It was early into the hike, but I had already given up on trying to be funny. I turned my focus to keeping one foot in front of the other.

Again, there were countless steps ahead of us on the trail. These were typically short logs situated sideways across the trail and were meant to assist hikers with the continuing uptick in elevation. With each step, my legs burned. These logs also served to divert the running water from the previous day's rain down the hill and off the trail.

"Fuck you," I heard Jeremy say from behind as he took a particularly steep step. "Fuck you. Fuck you. Fuck you."

This became our theme, our battle cry. My grunts and moans also became "fuck you" to the never-ending steps below my feet. We cursed each and every step.

Later that morning, we were passed by two other section hikers also heading south. It was the first time we had seen hikers tackling the southern portion of the trail alongside us. Their packs looked stout, even more so than ours, but the pair seemed to be moving along at a blistering pace. We chatted briefly and learned they would be staying at Tricorner Shelter that night, as well. Seeing other hikers cruising past us or down the hills coming from the south was frustrating. The will to move quickly was there, but my ability was sadly lacking.

I pushed on through my deteriorating pride and suffering.

An hour or so later we came to the top of a ridgeline and again found our new southbound friends. The pair had brought ultra-lightweight camping chairs with them and were enjoying the scenic views before continuing on to Tricorner. The flat area here offered a relatively good view of the mountains we had climbed earlier in the day. A few offshoot trails also converged at the intersection here.

Jeremy, Chris and I were again amazed by their pack sizes. Each of these two looked as though they were carrying seventy-five pounds inside eighty-liter backpacks.

While chatting, three older section hikers came from the south and stopped on the hill beside us.

"Be careful," one of the men warned. "There's a bear on the trail ahead. We didn't see it, but there's a ton of fresh scat all over the ground."

"We ran into two girls who saw a cub yesterday," I told them. "We didn't see it, but there's definitely bears out."

The older hikers were just finishing up their section hike of the Smokies and were on their way to Cosby Knob, which we had affectionately renamed Cosby's Knob earlier in the day.

We left and were passed by the southbound pair on the trail a short while later. They moved as though they had no weight on their backs and cruised past us again, seemingly hopping from stone to stair with each step up the mountain. It was again frustrating to see the pair moving so much more quickly than us.

As we settled into the last few hours of the hike, we came to a small flat area preceding another sharp incline up the mountain. I was hiking in front and stopped dead in my tracks by what was just ahead of us.

It was a bear, and it was massive.

The sight of a live bear in the woods, miles away from civilization and the possibility of a quick rescue, if necessary, petrified me. My stomach immediately sank, and I began to play through all of the lessons I had ever heard or read regarding a bear encounter.

Play dead?

No.

Run away?

No.

Charge the bear and attack before it had the chance to strike first?

Fuck no.

Jeremy began to turn to run away, but Chris and I both told him to stand his ground and to make as much noise as possible.

"Don't run!" Jeremy stopped before he could turn around.

"Hey bear!" I screamed. Jeremy and Chris did likewise. "Hey bear!" "Get out of here!" I heard from behind.

"Get!"

The noise did little to scare the bear as it began slowly lumbering toward us. We picked up rocks and tossed them onto the trail in front of the beast, but the stones were not effective. The bear kept coming. My aim was poor, and a good portion of the rocks I tossed toward the bear flew off into the woods alongside the trail.

"Shit!"

Eventually after a few more stones, one landed close enough in front that the bear stopped in its tracks and slowly crept up the hill on the right side of the path. We later joked that this was simply a minor inconvenience for the bear, but we had defeated it in combat nonetheless.

I kept my eyes on it as long as I could, but it eventually faded from view up the hill. As we approached the spot where the bear left the trail, we looked up and noticed it was sitting about ten yards up from us watching us pass by.

I couldn't help but put a human face and personality on the bear. It looked at us with a curious glance, like that of a dog hearing a strange noise for the first time.

We picked up more stones and yelled again. The bear remained steadfast. Eventually, I made a well-placed throw that hit a tree to the left of the bear. The sound startled it enough to cause it to continue up the mountain away from us. We quickly walked away. The bear did the same. We had survived our first bear encounter of the trip.

Despite near exhaustion and the excitement of the encounter wearing away our energy, we pushed on up the hill for fear of its return. After we were a hundred feet or more above the bear, we stopped to rest and to discuss what had just happened.

"Holy shit, that thing was huge," Chris said.

"At least four hundred pounds," Jeremy responded.

As we continued up the trail, the signs of scat were all along the path. The bear had obviously been walking the trail that morning scavenging for food. It was the bear's trail, and we were just borrowing it for the day.

The thrill of the encounter was not short-lived. We joked all morning about the bear attack and how we had actually beaten it in combat. We were reminded of scenes from The Revenant or Grizzly Man, thankful that our experience was pleasant by comparison.

Black bears are not as dangerous to humans as many hikers fear, but they should be respected and given plenty of space. The primary concern for bears is securing an easy meal, and attacking hikers for their backpacks is not easy. Unprovoked attacks by bears in the Smokies rarely happen, but the signs reminding park attendees to exercise caution were still everywhere.

We told everyone who passed us coming north about the bear. One older couple, Mr. and Mrs. Massachusetts as they were called, briefly stopped to chat after we told them what was up the trail.

"That bear has never hurt a hiker and a hiker has never hurt that bear," Mr. Massachusetts told us. "We'll be fine."

I was concerned about Mr. Massachusetts cavalier attitude, but he seemed old and wise enough to know a dangerous situation if and when one arose. He looked like the kind of man who would simply forgo throwing any stones or yelling and walk right up to a bear until it moved out of his way. He looked like a man with fortitude.

Hardly anyone we met had any real method of combating a bear. Our weapons were the size of our group and our voices. Only a few of the hikers we saw appeared to carry any bear mace or bear bells, and most of those hikers were hiking solo.

Later in the day, as the air began to chill, we met another thru-hiker while stopped at a trail intersection having an afternoon snack. Her name was M&M, and she was attempting a complete northbound hike of the Appalachian Trail.

"I quit my job and dropped out of college to do this," she told us somewhat embarrassingly as we snacked and rested. M&M had a thick southern accent that a young girl from Alabama or Mississippi might also have.

"Why do they call you M&M?" I asked in between gulps of water.

"It's not for the candy," she responded. "It stands for mind over matter."

"I think the candy is better," I told her only half joking.

M&M wore sandals instead of the more commonly used trail runners or hiking boots. This was because, as she said, her shoes gave her blisters when they were wet. She said her trail runners had been wet since the day she entered the Smokies, not surprising considering the amount of rain we experienced on our first day in the park. M&M told us the rain had been constant over the last few days. That was easy to believe judging by the continuous mud and running water along the pathway.

We talked about her trip, how long she had been on the trail, where she was from and what her plans were moving forward. I gave her my bag of trail mix and mixed nuts for the day, which she happily took. I joked that she was now my trail girlfriend.

"Yeah, okay," she sarcastically responded.

M&M seemed relieved to have a moment to rest on the trail, but she was obviously excited about being able to stay at the hostel in two days. She was tired, dirty and had the distinct smell of a hiker who had not showered in several days.

"Do they card for beer at Standing Bear?" she asked.

"You're not old enough to drink?" I quipped. "You're definitely my trail girlfriend now."

Jeremy and Chris found my overt creepiness hilarious. M&M, not so much.

We said our goodbyes, and M&M continued north as we strapped on packs back on and made our way south. Our short break was over, and we continued the march toward Tricorner Knob shelter.

As we often passed hikers coming north along the trail, we developed a pretty standard greeting for those we knew were not going to stop and talk to us. Most hikers preferred to keep moving, though sometimes there would be something interesting to briefly discuss, like a bear sighting or asking how far down the trail was the next shelter. For us, asking about the distance to the next shelter was common. The majority of my interactions on the trail were all basically the same.

"How's it going?"

"Good. You?"

"All right."

"Good hike!"

"Good hike!"

There were variations of our standard greeting, but more often than not, short and simple was best.

Several times we ran into a hiker that was literally running down the mountain, hopping and skipping with twenty or more pounds on their backs as they cruised down the rock-filled trail. These hikers had no time for us or anyone else on the trail for that matter. This was more common on our first two days as these hikers were primarily going downhill and were close to the end of the park.

Our second day of hiking turned out to be nearly as difficult as the first. My motivation was shot by the never-ending series of uphill climbs and the exhaustion of our bear encounter. The trail would climb, level off for a few feet, change direction and continue to climb. I later discovered this was the predominant setup for the entire trail through the Smokies. Before the hike, I knew there would be mountains to climb, I just had no idea there would be so many of them.

Thankfully, the shelter was only around eight miles from Cosby Knob. Our elevation gain the second day was around seventeen hundred feet, but added to the nearly four thousand feet we climbed the previous day, our legs and bodies began to break down well before the end of the second day's climb.

We finally arrived at the shelter in the late afternoon. We were some of the last hikers of the day to make it to the shelter. The two other southbound section hikers we met during the day were already at the shelter, and one was smoking a cigarette. He was my new best friend, even if he didn't know it yet.

I dropped my pack, went to the smoker first and pleaded for a cigarette. My packs were buried in my bag, and though I could have dug around, the need for instant gratification was very real. He happily obliged, and after a few puffs, I became dizzy with the sudden influx of nicotine in my system. I had already drastically cut down on the number of cigarettes I typically smoked per day while on the trail. I sat down on the ground next to the fire ring and watched the others eat while getting my fix.

Jeremy and Chris went off to set up their tents because the shelter was overcrowded and both were keen to have some peace and quiet away from the other hikers. I decided to push my luck and sleep inside, despite the lack of space on the wooden bunks.

The air that evening was chilly, and I worried the hammock would not provide enough protection from the cold. There was also a distinct lack of quality trees in the area to use as support for the hammock. A proper hammock setup requires two sturdy trees, more than a foot in diameter, spaced between ten and fifteen feet apart. Most of the trees at Tricorner Knob were clumped together in a close grouping that would have made setting up a hammock particularly difficult. Plus, by that point in the day, I was more concerned with immediate comfort and ease of sleep than with setting up and eventually tearing down the hammock. The very idea was laborious. We made our dehydrated dinners, shared stories, talked about our bear attack and made friends with a few of the hikers by giving away the rest of our day's food and sharing our vaporizers.

That night, we met two thru-hikers from the Atlanta area and talked about our hometown with fondness. For Jeremy, Chris and I, Atlanta was not some distant memory two hundred hiked miles away. We were just there a few days earlier.

After dinner, we discussed the next day. We would continue on to Pecks Corner and stay a day behind schedule. It was early enough in the hike that we hoped we could make up the lost time at some point moving forward, but we knew that our trip was already drastically different than our original outline. It now seemed unlikely that we would make our scheduled stop at Monte Le Conte Lodge for the hiker lunch or see several of the waterfalls north of the trail that we had marked as must-see landmarks in the weeks leading up to the hike. This also meant our planned distance would be cut from over one hundred miles to somewhere in the neighborhood of eighty.

All three of us were disappointed by the pace, which unfortunately continued to fall on my shoulders. I was the one most suffering up the hills. I was the one stopping to rest and catch my breath every chance I could get. I was the one holding up the entire group. If Jeremy or Chris were suffering, as well, they were doing a much better job of hiding it than I could. The hike was not easy for any of us, but it had been particularly difficult for me so far.

After Jeremy, Chris and most of the hikers had gone to sleep, I sat on a wooden bench outside of the shelter and puffed the last cigarette of the night while an older thru-hiker cooked his evening meal. I tried to make small talk, but he was disinterested in anything but his food. He ate noodles, a peanut butter tortilla, a pack of crackers and a few other small packages before going to bed himself.

As I sat on the bench outside of the shelter, I sighed in relief. The most difficult miles of our hike were now behind us. I turned in, looking forward to the lighter day to come.

Day Three
Swiss Cheese

I HAD SLEPT ON THE FLOOR of the Tricorner Knob shelter. Thru-hikers are required to use the shelters in the park, but if section hikers, like us, reserve a spot, the thru-hikers are expected to leave and set up a tent somewhere around the area of the building to make room. Since we had arrived at the shelter later in the afternoon, no one had offered to move out, but I didn't mind sleeping on the ground because it was softer than the wooden bunks. It was a nice change of pace, and I didn't want to inconvenience anyone who had already made their bed the night before.

That morning, I stirred awake and again was one of the last people in the shelter to wake up. I slept under the hanging packs and was probably a minor inconvenience to those packing up early in the morning. I found it hard to care about anyone else's time or plans.

Our hike that day would take us around five miles from Tricorner Knob Shelter to Pecks Corner, our shortest day of the trip so far. After climbing nearly six thousand feet and hiking close to twenty miles in two days, I welcomed the lighter, easier day.

Our original plan was to begin the third day at Pecks Corner and push on to Icewater Spring Shelter, but since that was now impossible, we stuck to our revised itinerary.

As I went to pack out that morning I noticed that one of the outside pockets had begun to rip away at the zipper. One of the thru-hikers saw this and joked about the condition of my Osprey backpack.

"Do you have a trail name yet?" he asked. "Because I'm going to call you Swiss Cheese since all of your gear has holes in it!"

It was a joke, but the joke stuck. I had gained a trail name thanks to my failing gear.

By this point in their thru-hike, almost all northbound hikers typically had trail names. Section hikers, like us, were never around the same group of people long enough to necessitate receiving one. Besides, we were walking in the other direction. We could have given them to ourselves, but that would have gone against the tradition of long distance backpacking.

Trail names were given out based on any number of reasons and primarily used to more easily remember people who are hiking the trail along with you. Sometimes a particular piece of gear or "luxury item" would determine a trail name. Sometimes it was food or some aspect of a hiker's physical appearance. Sometimes a trail name would be completely random with no obvious influences, like an inside joke that only a handful of hikers would ever know. There are a million different reasons why a hiker could be given a trail name. Mine happened to be because of a hole in a backpack.

Before the trip, I had fantasized about receiving an epic trail name, like something from Star Trek. Maybe Worf, since he was a cunning warrior and all around badass. Or maybe I would do something particularly clever and be given the name Spock. While Swiss Cheese was not at all epic, it was my name, and I accepted it with pride. Besides, it was better than Wheezy, Dead Legs, Slowpoke or any of the other trail names I actually deserved.

As we made our way through the park and met more thru-hikers, I began to notice a subtle divide between the thru-hikers and the section hikers that hadn't been immediately apparent from the onset. The vast majority of thru-hikers were pleasant and willing to share and enjoy the trail with us. A few, however, oozed an air of superiority over section and day hikers and either ignored or responded rudely when asked questions.

When we had arrived at the Tricorner Knob shelter the previous night, I encountered this for the first time. When one of the thru-hikers asked about our progress, we informed him that we had hiked about eight miles that day. He scoffed and said something underhanded about our lack of distance.

"Only eight miles?" he asked. "I do that before lunch."

"That's great," I sarcastically responded. What else could I say? Yes, we had been slow. Yes, I was physically beaten and battered. Yes, my morale was shot. Yep, you sure are a better backpacker than me! Good job, ass.

Another hiker commented, after asking about our day, that he hiked a minimum of twelve miles a day, regardless of terrain or condition.

Again, how were we supposed to respond to the smugness?

Much like life itself, there were people that we got along well with on the trail and others we did not. Thru-hikers had their own bond and brotherhood that tied them all together with the common goal of completing the entire twenty-one hundred mile long Appalachian Trail. Outsiders were simply not a part of that group until we had suffered the grind, as well. The Smoky Mountains were our adventure. To a thru-hiker, that section of the trail was just a small part of the experience. Hiking that alone would be an incomplete sense of the trail.

***

According to the Appalachian Trail Conservancy, the number of those attempting to complete the trail each year has risen almost one hundred percent in the last decade alone. The fact that many of the shelters where we stayed were packed from floor to ceiling proved that the promise of a long-distancing hiking adventure is more captivating today than ever before.

Unfortunately, most of these hikers will never make it to Mount Katahdin in Maine, the trail's eventual ending point. Before our hike, I had read that around thirty percent of everyone who starts out at Springer Mountain in Georgia would quit the trail at the first real stop, Neels Gap, just some thirty miles into the hike. If a third of all hikers fail before making it less than one percent through the trail, completing the entirety of the distance would be an amazing accomplishment.

More than half of everyone who starts the trail will not make it to the midway point at Harper's Ferry, Virginia. Nearly everyone else, more than seven out of ten hikers attempting the trail, fall off well before Maine for one reason or the other. Injury, money, time and life's unexpected surprises are some of the reasons why even hikers with the best intentions fail to finish the entire trail. Even famed travel writer, Bill Bryson, who wrote about his hike in the book "A Walk in the Woods", only made it partially through the trail. His story has become the go-to novelization of life on the trail, and even he failed.

It's possible, one thru-hiker told me, to go for days in the latter half of the Appalachian Trail without seeing or camping with anyone else. The odds of actually finishing would not be in their favor.

The previous summer, I had taken my daughter hiking in North Georgia and stopped at Neels Gap to check out the hostel and outfitters store there. The shop is a surprisingly well-equipped outfitter, just three days from the official starting point at Springer Mountain for those hiking north.

Several trees line the property at Neels Gap, and dozens of pairs of boots, trail runners and tennis shoes hung from the trees. This was either an admission of defeat or a warning for those who decide to continue the walk to Maine. I guess that varies on perspective.

Odds are nearly everyone, no matter how confident, smug, humble, healthy or unhealthy, will fail. That's the challenge that draws many to attempt the trail and is the greatest motivator.

There are as many different kinds of hikers are there are people. We met young kids, fresh from high school looking for a pre-college challenge. We met middle-aged men and women who had always dreamed of hiking the trail but had never completed the hike for whatever reason. There were older men and women who had been hiking their entire lives. Some were completing the Smoky Mountains section for the second or third time. Some were completing the entire trail for the second or third time.

Some backpackers we met were well-to-do. Some probably had no home to go to once they had completed the trail. The mix of class and money is evident throughout, but unimportant to the overall experience. Ultralight, expensive gear doesn't matter if you can't make it up and down the hills when you're too overweight or out of shape.

Nothing would matter if you rolled your ankle or twisted your knee on a particularly difficult section. The mountains had a natural way of leveling the playing field. No amount of gear alone could prepare a person for the constant up and down of the mountains. Once a hiker begins the trail, the stamina they gain from the daily grind becomes the most important factor. Sustaining that stamina and staying determined were the only true allies to a long distance hiker.

It's not uncommon for hikers to begin the trail at Springer Mountain only being able to physically hike a few short miles per day. The pack weight and adjustments to the body take a while to work through.

Many hikers say that it takes around two hundred miles on the trail before they are completely comfortable with their "trail legs" and are able to grind out the necessary miles per day to make it to Maine within the required timeline. This puts that two hundred mile tally right around the middle of the Great Smoky Mountains National Park. By the time we were meeting hikers, they had just become fully comfortable with maintaining and increasing their daily progress. They were also fairly confident about what was in their packs and how best to carry it.

Most hikers figure out very early on that weight and excess gear is a detriment, often mailing back unused or unnecessary gear at the first chance they come across. Even section hikers will sometimes stop and mail excess food or supplies back home once they realize they're carrying useless pounds. We might have done this if we had come across a place to do so, as the food weight in my pack seemed never-ending.

Hiking the trail can be relatively expensive if comfort and sustaining a diet are important to the hiker. Packs, gear, water filtration, food, permits, the occasional stop at a hostel or town for a rest day and replacements or repairs of gear quickly add up. Some hikers are able to handle the financial burden better than others thanks to support from families or trust funds. Some hikers buy the cheapest possible gear and accept handouts along the way while staying in town or a hostel as infrequently as possible. We saw both extremes.

It's possible, though extremely difficult, to hike the entire trail staying only at the shelters. Some hikers have chosen to go the entire distance without carrying a tent, hammock or even a tarp to sleep under. The Appalachian Trail has somewhere around two hundred and fifty shelters; some are more elaborate than others but all serve the same purpose of keeping hikers warm and dry while providing a place to sleep.

Shelters in the park typically consisted of three stone walls, with two layers of wooden bunks inside, a small fireplace and dirt floor. Though not glamorous in the least, these shelters were well-built and quite comfortable in the rain and snow, especially when the large tarps were covering the sleeping area. Most of the shelters in the park had gone through a refurbishment in recent years. It was evident that quite a bit of care had gone into maintaining the shelters.

For several years, the shelters had chain-link fences to protect hikers from bears and other creatures of the night. Renovations to shelters up and down the trail, including installing steel bear cables to hang food and packs, and more education directed toward hikers meant that fences were no longer needed.

We arrived early enough in the spring that nearly all of the shelters on the north side of Clingman's Dome still had large tarps over the sleeping areas. These were particularly helpful in staying warm on the nights when there was snow, sleet, freezing rain or blasts of freezing air circling around outside.

Most shelters featured some kind of wood bench or table in the front-half of the shelter. Often, there was a wooden table on the side of the shelter, as well. The shelters along the Appalachian Trail in the Smokies generally slept twelve to sixteen hikers, but many more could fit on the two bunks if hikers didn't mind sleeping immediately beside one another.

All of the shelters we came across were littered with graffiti. This bothered some hikers more than others. I saw the graffiti markings and signatures as tainting the overall natural experience. Jeremy and Chris didn't mind the markings nearly as much as I did.

Some of the graffiti was actually clever but not always. Often, I'd look up to see someone had scribbled something as ridiculous as "Wolfpack 420" on the rafters, high above the shelter floor. As with urban graffiti, the better the quality, the less I cared about its presence. One shelter had "Jon Snow Lives" scribbled on the wall above the outside picnic table well before HBO's big Game of Thrones reveal.

Sometimes, there were motivational sayings on the shelter walls. One stated simply: "Don't let the hiking get in the way of the hike." This was my favorite. I kept this phrase in my head as we progressed through the park as an ever-present reminder to enjoy the adventure as much as I could, regardless of the difficulties immediately facing me. This was sometimes easier than others.

It had been my dream for several years to complete the entire trail in one passing. The hike typically takes around six months, though some hikers are able to finish in a far quicker time than others. The reality of adulthood, a job, having a child and other real life responsibilities were now my barriers to completing the entire trail at this point in my life.

Perhaps one day in the future, maybe during my retirement, I would be able to complete the trail. But, as I slugged along uphill sections,

I wondered if completing the trail would even be something I'd want to do later in life.

Jeremy and Chris felt likewise.

"I don't think I'd even want to do the entire trail," Jeremy told us during our walk to the next shelter that day. "It would just seem so boring. If it's just walking in the woods for two thousand miles, why not just do the cool parts and skip all the bullshit?"

Jeremy had a point. Of course, the trail had hundreds of interesting landmarks and sights littered up and down the path. There were long stretches in the Smokies that were nothing more than walking up and down mountain after mountain in the woods. Often, there were no views, no streams or waterfalls to distract us from the monotony of the hike. When the views did come, it made the effort and exhaustion worth it, but those were certainly not constant.

***

That afternoon, as we were climbing a particularly difficult uphill section, Chris shouted from behind that a group of hikers were coming up from the north end of the trail. We paused for a moment to let the group pass.

This group consisted of four older men and women, all wearing daypacks. They were doing a section between Pecks Corner and Cosby Knob and were racing up the hill as if being chased by a black bear. The sight of hikers, possibly as old as my grandparents, crushing the uphill was disheartening. Even if they weren't carrying the same kind of weight we were, their pace was impressive and not just impressive for their combined age, which was well over two hundred years. I hung my head in shame as they passed.

One of the men stopped briefly to chat. "They're calling for snow in the higher elevations in the park tomorrow," the old man said. He was obviously thrilled to be in the woods. His excitement was palpable.

"Snow?"

"Yep! It's supposed to start overnight and continue into Thursday. Good hike!"

"Good hike," I begrudgingly responded.

A short while later, another group of elderly hikers again passed us, but this time from the rear. They, too, were wearing daypacks and were also hiking at least twice our speed up the hill.

Eventually, as we continued upward, we came to a short, flat area and began a steady decline. I heard Jeremy shout from behind.
"God damn, that one's got a fucking bear claw!"

An older woman came up the hill toward us. In her right hand were her hiking poles. In her left, a large bear claw pastry. She was pushing toward the top of the ridge while munching feverously on the treat.

"Don't worry, I'm not a bear," she shouted back with a smile, seemingly unaware of Jeremy's colorful description of the situation. Perhaps she had heard and simply ignored it.

We continued on, shamed by our lack of pace compared to the older hikers we saw on the trail that day. Jeremy and Chris less so than me. They were stuck with me after our disastrous first day, promising to stay as a group for the remainder of the hike, no matter how slowly I crawled or held them off their ideal pace. My effort at times must have frustrated them, but they didn't complain.

As we approached the next shelter, Pecks Corner, we came to a junction in the trail. The shelter was nearly a half-mile off of the Appalachian Trail to the south, down an easy decline.

Sometimes, we would hike for hours and only cover a few miles. Sometimes we could do two or three miles in an hour if the terrain was favorable. Walking down to Pecks Corner felt like an instant, and before we knew it, we had arrived at the shelter and were already setting up for the night. We often joked that signs in the park were simply estimations of distance and not the actual number of miles or tenths of a mile. At least, in this case, the estimate was in our favor.

Trails can change over time, and the Appalachian Trail, in particular, is never exactly the same from one season to the next. Downed trees and other obstacles mean that no two people will ever hike the exact same hike, even if they walk together.

When we arrived at Pecks Corner, there were already three or four people at the shelter. Because we had only hiked five or so miles, it was early and the sun was still shining. Jeremy, Chris and I were able to find bunk spaces without any issue and set about drying our clothes in the sun from the previous rainy days. I hung two pairs of socks, underwear and my boots on a tree in the direct sunlight. Chris and Jeremy both unwrapped their tents and found places to hang those, as well.

"My two-pound tent weighs ten pounds," Jeremy joked, as unfolded his tent onto a bush.

We made a good time that day, but our distance was shorter than any day we had planned during the entire trip. We were still a day behind schedule, and the possibility of snow flurries coming the next day meant that we could be pushed even further back if the weather so decided. None of us wanted to take another day to finish, which meant we had to prepare ourselves for the possibility of pushing through inclement weather. Still, I was not yet convinced that any substantial amount of snow would actually fall on us.

That afternoon as the sun moved toward the horizon, a nice variety of hikers made their way to the shelter. Several younger thru-hikers showed up, and a few older, more seasoned hikers joined, as well. The older hikers grouped together to share their experiences and largely left the younger adventurers alone.

One hiker, named Legs, had just returned to the trail after traveling to Austin, Texas on a Greyhound for a week to attend a music festival that was eventually canceled. His spirits were high, however, and he was happy to be back on the trail with fresh supplies and a bag of cheap weed that he happily shared with anyone who asked.

"Why do they call you Legs?" I asked.

"Because I have fantastic legs!" he responded with a smile. "Actually, I didn't bring any pants with me on the trail. I'm hoping that decision isn't a bad one if it snows tomorrow." Legs had hiked the entire trail so far, from Georgia to the Smokies, wearing only shorts.

By late afternoon, the clouds had rolled through the mountaintops and the rain had mostly stopped. The air began to chill but still felt too warm to actually snow. I could imagine a bit of sleet or frozen rain in the morning before the sun blasted the mountaintops in the afternoon, but snow? That couldn't happen.

We dubbed one Canadian hiker at Pecks Corner John Madden because his commentary and advice were painfully obvious to anyone that had ever been camping or hiking before. He had a knack for awkwardly interjecting advice in completely unrelated conversations.

"If you're cold, the best way to get warm is to climb in your sleeping bag wearing a few dry layers," he told a group of chilly thru-hikers as the sun was setting. "Be sure to hang your food from the bear cable and not the hooks on the line since the bears can swat the lines and get the bags to drop if they're not properly secure. If you want your clothes to get dry, hang them up in direct sunlight when you get to a shelter."

Many hikers on the trail were quick to offer advice on how best to do something. Once, while hiking up a particularly large hill, a hiker had passed by us and commented on how Chris was holding his hiking poles.

"It really helps if you push them down in the ground when you walk."

"Thanks, but I've got a good thing going here," Chris responded far more diplomatically than I ever could.

After a few moments up the trail and out of earshot, Chris sounded off. "What the hell? Does he think I'm not putting the poles on the ground? What an idiot!"

"I hope he feels like an ass," Jeremy said.

Chris' poles and how they were being used was a running joke for the remainder of the hike.

At Standing Bear Farms a few days earlier, one hiker had suggested that I cut weight by carrying only four ounces of water during our time in the park since there were a plethora of water sources.

"There are enough water sources in the mountains that you never have to worry about it," he had stated confidently.

As we later found out, that was definitely not the case. But we didn't take his advice either, because, well, it was bad. Sure, there is water on and around the trail in many places, but there's no way anyone should carry only four ounces while hiking. An emergency alone could necessitate having a minimum of two liters on you at any given time. I preferred to begin my days with at least that much water. Even day hikers, only trekking a few miles on a well-traveled trail should carry far more than four ounces at a time. We weren't trying to break any speed records, we simply wanted to survive the experience.

Some of the advice we received was actually pretty good. One hiker suggested that we wear wet and damp clothes on top of dry clothes while we slept. The heat from our bodies would help dry out the wet articles. This was something I ended up doing several times during the hike, even though it made my sleeping bag liner and the inside of my sleeping bag smell like a decaying corpse.

Another hiker suggested that we sleep on the top bunk of the shelter if rain was in the forecast. This would help us avoid water leakage from the top if it was particularly wet and late arrivals climbed up to the top bunk without stripping off their wet layers first. Also good advice.

A common saying on the trail is "hike your own hike." This typically applies to the gear, fitness and how a hiker chooses to put his or her two feet in front of themselves with each and every step. Everyone has a different and unique approach. It makes no sense to expect someone else to conform to another style of hiking simply because it worked for them.

Of the three of us, Chris brought the most seemingly unnecessary gear. His trowel was military grade and came with a pick-axe, saw attachment and folded into a clever, albeit heavy, little ball of twisted metal. He brought an entire roll of duct tape, enough to completely repair the damaged gear for everyone on the entirety of the Appalachian Trail. Chris also had two cans of bug spray and many, many pairs of socks. How his pack was able to accommodate all of the extras he brought with him was beyond me.

Jeremy and I had been a bit more pragmatic with our gear selections, but as we neared the midpoint of our trip, I found myself wondering what I could have cut from my weight, as well. I had not used my knife, compass, rope, wood-burning stove or much of the trinkets I brought with me that was not directly used for eating, sleeping or walking. While Chris' gear was bulky and heavy, at least he was using most of it.

That afternoon, once most of the hikers had arrived, we cooked our dehydrated meals. I had brought with me a wood stove, but almost all of the available twigs and small sticks were still soaked through and would not burn. Jeremy and Chris were kind enough to let me use their propane stoves, and I had brought a small canister of fuel with me just in case the wood stove plan fell through. It was wishful thinking on my part, but I was happy to have a backup plan just in case. I used the propane stoves as often as Jeremy and Chris.

The propane stove canisters seemed to last forever. So much so, that Chris had used his stove to dry out his trail runners on several occasions.

That evening, several of the hikers shared their extra food. One hiker opened a Toblerone candy bar and snapped off pieces for anyone who asked. I gave away my trail mix while another hiker shared her chocolate candy, as well. It was a venerable feast in the forest, one in which I was more than happy to take part. Another hiker broke out a joint, lifting my spirits even further.

Weed is fairly prevalent on the trail. Even if the majority of hikers don't smoke themselves, pot is accepted as a part of trail life for thru-hikers, section hikers and even many of the younger day hikers. I hadn't regularly smoked marijuana in several years, but this trip was different. I knew I wanted to take something with me that would calm me down and offer a bit of enjoyment after the end of long days. Booze, as fun as it can be, was not at all what I wanted to consume vast amounts of in bear country after a long day of hiking. Plus, whiskey bottles or flasks are heavy.

Jeremy and I had both brought with us small vaporizer pens with cartridges filled with condensed marijuana oil. These vaporizer pens offer all the benefits of smoking pot, mostly getting high to relax the mind and body, without some of the drawbacks like smell and pack space. The vapor produced by the oil was nearly odorless, at least more so than smoking a joint or pipe would have been. This was important to us, as we hoped to avoid irritating anyone's sensibilities or running into trouble with a ranger should we encounter one. The pen and capsules were also relatively small and light.

We puffed on these pens quite a bit before falling asleep at night in the shelters. Jeremy would lay in his sleeping bag on the bunk, toking away while watching whatever movie he had prepped for the night. Chris and I would smoke, as well, while listening to music or simply enjoying the quiet stillness. It would have been easy to justify smoking as some kind of excuse to get stoned in the woods, but in truth, it had a million benefits.

"That's one of the great things about being a section hiker, you get to bring along some pretty cool toys," one hiker told us.

Besides the obvious effects of smoking pot after each day's hike, the marijuana had other pluses. Pain management, aiding in sleep and opening up another avenue for socializing also came along with puffing the pens. A few times we exchanged pen hits for actual, real-life puffs on rolled J's or someone's one-hitter.

My vaporizer held up fairly well considering the moisture and wetness I experienced on the first day. At no point during the trip did the vaporizer fail or even consider not working as intended. Even in the blistering cold of a nineteen-degree night, the pen worked like a charm.

The hikers that did not smoke never seemed bothered by us doing it, and even if most hikers did not carry any with them while hiking, many accepted a puff or two at night in the shelters. Sharing the pen became a way of finding like-minded hikers. It also opened up a social aspect on the trail that I had not expected. It made us part of the "cool" crowd.

Though some hikers have undoubtedly hiked the Appalachian Trail while using more illicit, harmful drugs, we never saw any indication that anyone else was using anything more potent. Hiking the trail was not conducive to doing party drugs. I couldn't imagine trying to maintain a drug habit while on the trail for any lengthy period of time.

One hiker told us of her friend, who received a pound of marijuana through a mail drop toward the beginning of the trail. She was selling the pot, dime bag at a time, to fund her trip, something I imagined quite a few hikers have done over the years.

The crowd at Pecks Corner was the most interesting and diverse group we had encountered so far. We chatted after dinner about everything from trail conditions to our hometowns. I puffed on my vaporizer pen until the sun went down.

For the first time during our hike, all three of us decided to sleep in the shelter. It was crowded, but not overly so as several of the thru-hikers chose to set up tents around the shelter instead of sleeping on the bunks. I laid down and closed my eyes to the whipping cold outside, thankful for the large tarps that covered the missing fourth wall.

I fell asleep that night to the sound of light rain against the metal roof and Chris' ever-present snoring.

Day Four
Enter the Icebox

WE AWOKE AT PECKS CORNER to the sound of frozen rain slamming against the thin metal roof above us. In a strange way, the small ice drops hitting against the aluminum roof above were calming and peaceful from inside our sleeping bags. The cold wind outside provided a brief glimpse into the day to come, and the realization that our day would be the coldest one so far soon followed. It took an incredible amount of willpower to get out of the sleeping bag that morning. I could have stayed bundled up all day.

Packing away our gear before setting off had become much easier each day. I was three days down on food, and my pack had lost almost six pounds by this point. It was a noticeable difference. I was still carrying more food than I would eat every day, and I knew this, but it was getting a little easier to pull up and strap on the pack each morning. Even with my Swiss cheese backpack, every day had become easier than the day before.

The hike today would take us a little over seven miles south to Icewater Springs shelter. Along the way, we would see Charlies Bunion, one of the most famous landmarks in the entire Great Smoky Mountains National Park.

The sleet continued to rain down on the shelter as we ate breakfast and packed up our gear. Soon after eating, we set off again back toward the trail. The previous day, we hiked down nearly half a mile to Pecks Corner from the actual Appalachian Trail. This hike, entirely downhill, was a breeze. The hike out was relatively easy, despite the uphill. We were getting better, faster and stronger.

My legs, despite the ever-present soreness, worked best in the early mornings. After an hour or two, I would find myself again struggling up the inclines, but today was different. Today was the first day my battered body fully accepted the punishment, and I was able to deal with the inclines without too much suffering.

The sleet continued to rain down on us as we walked under the canopy, but the precipitation slowly turned into white, fluffy snow. Eventually, the trees and bushes began to collect the powder. It felt like Christmas. In May. It was Christmas in fucking May.

"Let's hear those sleigh bells ring-a-ling, ding ding ding-a-ling dong," I sang as we made our way through the slush and falling snow. If it looked like Christmas, it should sound like Christmas, too, I thought.

"Are you singing fucking Christmas music?" Chris shouted from the back.

"It's lovely weather for a snow hike together with you!"

Chris suffered from tinnitus and told us he often used music as a way to help cope with the constant ringing in his ears, particularly when he tried to sleep at night. He also had the misfortune of easily getting a song stuck in his head, something I playfully took advantage of several times during the hike.

I stopped often and grabbed snow from the leaves and ate them like ice chips. By this point in the hike, I had completely given up on trying to drink through my Camel bag stuffed in my pack. I had begun filtering water straight from my Smart water bottles and craved a full bottle to down in a few gulps without having to suck through a tube or the end of my filter.

The snow continued to fall throughout the morning. Eventually, the sleet disappeared completely as we made our way closer to Charlies Bunion. The snow gathered alongside the trail, in the trees, and on our bodies.

Dressing in layers was key. In total, I had five layers of clothing on my top and two and a half on my legs. I wore a long sleeve microfiber shirt under a short sleeve shirt. Over both of those, I wore a button up shirt. On top of that was a puffy jacket and over everything was my trusted poncho. On my legs, I wore thermal underwear under my pants and nearly knee-high socks. Despite the layers, I was still cold whenever we stopped for too long.

The benefit was that none of us were sweating much and did not require nearly as much water during the hike.

***

The sign leading to the Charlies Bunion loop trail reads simply, "Charlies Bunion -- Control Your Children." Only 0.1 miles stands between Appalachian Trail hikers and the large rock outcrop, and this area is as popular with Appalachian Trail thru-hikers as it is day hikers and tourists as it loops from one point on the trail to another in a relatively short and quick space.

When we arrived from the north, the Charlies Bunion loop trail immediately changed from a soft, dirt path with light stones and roots to a completely rocky, boulder-filled trail. The snow was falling heavily and the sky was nearly completely gray as we slowly made our way up the rocky trail. We carefully hiked up the trail toward the top of the mountain, not entirely sure what to expect from the climb. The cold, wet rock below our feet offered little traction as the snow continued to fall around us.

A few days earlier, a thru-hiker was showing everyone in the shelter his photos from Charlies Bunion. Jeremy, Chris and I refused to look. Why spoil the coming experience by looking through the lens of someone else's camera when we were only a few days away?

Large boulders and the rocky cliff were to our left. On the right, just a few feet away, was a drastic fall from the trail to the floor of the valley below. Because of the impaired view thanks to the snow and gray backdrop, we had no idea just how far below the valley below would go down, but we later learned that Charlies Bunion was well over five thousand feet above sea level. A fall here would likely have been deadly.

Stone summits in the Smokies were rare. The entire summit of Charlies Bunion was rock, save a few small plants and grasses here and there. The views here were among the best in the park, apparently. We were unable to experience this as the snow blanketed the rock and the gray backdrop dulled the sky around us. Maybe we should have looked at the thru-hiker's photos after all.

How the mountain came to be called Charlies Bunion is still debated to this day. What is known is that the mountain was named by author and explorer Horace Kephart after one of his companions, Charlie Conner, and was later certified by the United States Geological Survey as Charlies Bunion. The name alone suggests that Charlie, at some point during his adventures with Kephart, had a rather gnarly podiatric problem that was worthy of the history books.

Once we arrived at the high point of the Charlies Bunion loop trail, we paused for several moments to breathe in the majestic stone summit and to take a few photos. The gray backdrop against the near-black stone made this section of trail feel shockingly different than any previous section we had come across. It was like we had transported to the surface of a Ridley Scott-inspired alien planet for a few brief moments. The wind whipped us from the valley below.

The three of us spent several moments posing against the rock face, taking every kind of photo imaginable. The views of the mountains and valleys below were legendary, but we could see only gray.

Soon after, the cold began to set in and we continued our trek to Icewater Springs shelter. Everyone we ran into on the trail that day called the shelter the "Icebox" and for good reason. Once we arrived, the snow had accumulated to several inches and the wind was blowing fairly heavily up the ridge and inside the shelter. There was very little warmth to be found there that evening.

Though we were some of the first hikers to arrive that day, another group was there, as well. They had used their rainflies and tarps to make a homemade wind-blocking system. I added my hammock rainfly to the mix on the bottom bunk and unpacked my gear. It felt nice to have a use for the hammock equipment after several days of rain, snow and no suitable trees to swing from.

Over the next hour or so, a slow trickle of people arrived at the shelter.

John Boy and Billy Bob, two middle-aged hikers from southern Mississippi, stumbled into the shelter just before dusk covered in powdered snow and visible misery. I dubbed them after two southern radio personalities who hosted a syndicated radio show across the southeast thanks to their fantastical southern accents. They had hiked all day in the weather, and John Boy stood under the snow-covered roof of the shelter for several moments with a look of wintry shock on his face.

Again, there was actually snow in fucking May.

John Boy was dressed in a head-to-toe rain suit and was shivering as he brushed the powder from his shoulders and pack. Once he warmed up, he happily told us his story.

"I broke my back last year," he said. "And I got two screws in my knee. I figured what better way to rehab than go hiking the trail?"

"That's pretty intense man," I responded.

"Oh yeah. I came out here back on Easter, and there was snow everywhere. I just couldn't do it, man."

John Boy had attempted the Great Smoky Mountain National Park Appalachian Trail section a few months earlier over the Easter holidays but was unable to complete the hike due to the cold and the weather. For his second attempt, he brought along Billy Bob and was determined to finish the park on his second try.

The pair told us that they were doing the same section of trail that we were, but they had started further into the park than we had done just a few days earlier since John Boy had already completed the earlier portion. The duo was the first pair we had met that was attempting the entire park north to south. We shared much of the same schedule, planning to be at the same shelters several more times before the end of the hike. It was refreshing to meet other southbound section hikers. The duo had become our competition, the benchmark which would compare ourselves to for the remainder of the week.

Billy Bob was more quiet and reserved than his boisterous friend. It was obvious both were outdoorsmen, hikers, hunters and fisherman in their free time. John Boy was loud, excitable and seemingly more fun than his friend.

That day, May 5, was also Cinco de Mayo. The cold and snow, in combination with the most American of Mexican holidays, meant that a few sips of whiskey were in order. Chris had brought with him a pint of Woodland Reserve and Jameson. He had given me the bottle of Jameson to consume before we even left Standing Bear Farms, but I'm sure cutting the weight of a glass bottle filled with booze from his pack was a pleasant byproduct of the gesture.

We shared our whiskey with John Boy and Billy Bob, and they, in turn, shared their rum with us. The booze certainly helped warm our cold and tired bones, and it was nice to celebrate Cinco de Mayo far away from civilization without the roar of obnoxious suburbanites drinking margaritas and eating tacos.

The whiskey was delicious. Initially, the thought of getting drunk in the evenings, far away from the outside world after a day's hike was unappealing. The three of us actually thought we would carry the bottles with us until the bitter end, perhaps celebrating the night before our hike out. But tonight, the cold had necessitated the warmth of liquor. With each sip, I could feel my insides burn. There may have been snow on the ground, but my belly warmed my body.

One hiker arrived later that evening wearing no shoes at all. He must have been miserable in the cold snow. Two other hikers offered to let him warm his feet on their dehydrated meals. Nothing about that seemed right to me. The hiker was an older, gray man with a stony facial expression and wrinkled body. He had somehow made it through the snow, sleet and up and down the endless rock and root-covered mountains and hills wearing nothing on his feet.

Late arrivals to the shelter were disappointed with the fact that some of the other hikers did not want to share their rainflies or move their tarps around to help the others block out the wind. We did our best to accommodate, but that meant little. That evening, a few of the thru-hikers decided to brave the snow and ice to build a fire inside the shelter.

Several of the hikers trekked off into the woods around the shelter to find dried, burnable wood. The snow and ice had done its part in bringing down the dead and dying limbs, but none of the wood brought back into the shelter was anywhere close to dry.

The effort of sustaining the fire must have kept a few of the others warm, but the fire itself died just an hour or so after everyone had laid down to sleep. The fire had done little to warm the inside of the uncovered shelter.

Two northbound thru-hikers, both younger kids, stayed awake much later than everyone else laughing and talking about video games, hiking and their future plans on the trail. One-half of the pair, a young girl, was obviously enamored with her hiking counterpart. He, sadly, seemed disinterested in her romantic advances.

"I think we should do the four state challenge," she told him.

"I don't know if we'll even be in the same place by then," he responded coldly.

One of the other hikers made a comment after laying down that the kids below were hosting their own radio show for everyone to hear. The girl didn't seem to understand this was a backhanded request for the pair to quiet down. She laughed.

"Haha! We have our own radio show! Haha!"

She continued to sell her partner on the idea of hiking together until the end of the trail.

The four state challenge takes hikers through four states in twenty-four hours: Virginia, West Virginia, Maryland and Pennsylvania.

Other unofficial hikes on the trail include the half gallon of ice cream at the halfway challenge, Hike Naked Day or the 24x24x24 challenge, where hikers drink twenty-four beers while hiking twenty-four miles in twenty-four hours.

For hikers making it that far into the journey, boredom and monotony take full hold. It's the little things, like those challenges, that keeps the hike fresh and interesting to some after a thousand miles, especially when the majority of their friends and fellow hikers fall off the trail.

The girl went on and on well into the night.

Earplugs had become a necessity on the trail. Sharing a sleeping space with a new group of strangers every night meant that a sound and restful night's sleep was never guaranteed. Chris snored throughout the night. I snored. At times, it must have seemed like a symphony of nasally apnea breathing for any light sleepers in the shelters where we slept.

I laid in my sleeping bag staring at the wooden bunk floor above me until drifting off to sleep to the muffled sounds of cackling beside me while the snow outside continued to collect.

Day Five
Minister Gem

SLEEPING IN THE SHELTERS was miserably uncomfortable. In addition to the hard, wooden flooring, space inside was cramped and some of the hikers, myself included, snored throughout each night. Sleeping in the Icebox was by far the worst night of the hike so far. The wind coming over the ridge poured into the shelter like an old motel air conditioning unit blasting out cold air with a broken off switch.

Because we had fashioned our own tarp system that only covered a section of the lower bunk the day before, cracks in the tarps allowed cold air to flow in all night. Luckily, we were on the bottom and the tarps at least covered the space between the floor and top bunk. Anyone who slept on the top bunk the night before had half as much coverage as we did and must have been even more miserable during the night than those of us on the bottom.

I had tossed and turned. I switched from side to side, stomach to back, back to side consistently. Once the pain on my hips became too much to stand, I'd flip over again. I woke up more than a dozen times attempting to get comfortable. Nothing I tried worked and eventually I settled on being both cold and in pain.

My sleeping pad, a folding Thermarest foam pad, was about as thick as my thumb when completely laid out. I was usually able to fold the top few sections back on itself to create a little pillow for myself. It wasn't much, but it did help slightly. I had also used my puffy jacket as extra padding for my head, balling it up and stuffing the body and sleeves into one of the pockets. It actually worked.

I had slept in three layers. My larger sleeping bag, probably the single largest item in my backpack, might have been big, but it was not warm. I stuffed a sleeping bag liner inside of a summer sleeping bag I had also brought with me. The three layers together proved to be more than sufficient for the cold against my body, and that morning, for the first time, I was not regretting the decision of stuffing something extra in my backpack.

The dry, snowy air and miserable night's sleep made the next morning very difficult. Finding the strength to get out of the sleeping bag, putting on layer after layer of clothing and strapping on my cold and wet boots was not easy. Our food bags hung the night before from the steel bear cables next to the shelter, were covered in ice. Inside, nearly everything with a soft consistency had frozen solid.

Eventually, I mustered the energy to begin the day. We packed up the gear, ate and eventually said our goodbyes to our shelter mates. John Boy and Billy Bob slept in that day, but the pair was scheduled to meet us at the next shelter, Mt. Collins.

We decided the goal for the day was to beat John Boy and Billy Bob to Mt. Collins. We had the advantage of time and youth on our side, but both men, from what we had seen the day before and despite John Boy's recent injuries, were more than capable hikers. We also had the benefit of an early start. Both men were still sound asleep when we left the shelter a little before nine.

Mt. Collins shelter was just over seven miles down the trail, but the major landmark of the day was Newfound Gap. Here, we would cross the only road that passed over the Appalachian Trail in the entire park, US Route 441.

Newfound Gap was around three miles into our day, which meant we'd have the opportunity for a nice break after a bit of fast-paced downhill hiking. Though we began the day with a short uphill section, most of the following three miles were a manageable decline.

The cold, wet air meant a steady stream of snot came from my nose as we continued our walk through the Appalachian Winter Wonderland. I wore one of my many handkerchiefs around my neck and used it to constantly wipe the moisture from my face. My beard caught most of the drainage, but the cold numbed the feeling in my face. I was certain that I would have frozen goop on my face until the sun came back to warm the mountains.

The three of us began to separate slightly as we made our way down the hill toward Newfound Gap. This portion of the trail was full of early morning day hikers and even some families. I came across couples, families and even solo hikers as they made their way up the mountain back toward Charlies Bunion.

I upped my pace even more and cruised to the bottom of the hill far more quickly than Jeremy or Chris, encouraged by an actual bathroom and trash receptacle by the road. At this point in the hike, I had accumulated at least a pound of garbage, conveniently stored in a gallon Ziploc bag on the outside of my pack. It smelled bad, was heavy and took up valuable space in my outside pocket. I wanted it gone.

Losing any weight, particularly smelly food wrappers and old, wet cigarette butts, was welcome. Freeing up space was also crucial. My pack had developed another rip and one of my exterior pockets was quickly becoming useless.

When I arrived at Newfound Gap, the sea of tourists and visitors blew me away. I had only been away from civilization, but this experience already felt strange.

Jeremy and Chris had fallen off my pace and were pretty far behind me by the time I reached the bottom of the hill. I went to the bathroom in an actual restroom and smoked a cigarette while waiting for my compatriots to come down the hill. Eventually, the pair made it, and we met beside the road next to the parking lot to take in the sights.

Seeing the tourists at Newfound Gap was a shock. For days, we had been hiking in the presence of mostly fit, thin, disgusting and exhausted backpackers. There were no cars, no fumes, no buses or crowds of people clamoring over each other for the best view or spot to snap a selfie at the shelters or on the trail. At most, there were a dozen or so hikers at a shelter. All of them, regardless of how far they were hiking or where they were going, were like me. The people at Newfound Gap were different.

Here, dozens of tourists walked around the parking lot looking for the best views to pose for photos. We stopped and sat on a rock wall overlooking a never-ending series of mountain ranges below. The fumes from the cars idling next to us were nauseating. We had been there only a short while, but I already missed the quiet stillness of the trail and the smell of clean air.

The three of us were an oddity. Some of the tourists commented on our appearance while others were curious about our trip. Others simply sneered as they walked past, probably disgusted with our hiker stench. Our collective odor would not have made us any friends.

"Are you hiking the trail?" an older man asked as he and his wife walked past. We sat against our packs, resting on the half stone wall and enjoying the views in the cool breeze.

"Sure are! Just the section through the park, though. We're only going about eighty miles going north to south."

"Wow! That's great. Well, good luck to you!"

A few other groups made similar comments. It felt as though many of the people we spoke with that afternoon were living vicariously through our experience.

At the gap, the views were fantastic, but the wind whipped over the treeless hills without hesitation. While it was nice to break and rest for a moment, the chill and car fumes became too much to contend with, and we eventually set off again.

Newfound Gap is about as close to the center of the Great Smoky Mountains National Park as you can get. To the north is Gatlinburg, Tennessee and to the south is Cherokee, North Carolina. Many thru-hikers take a day of rest and resupply in Gatlinburg.

Gatlinburg has a reputation for being a tourist trap with expensive hotels and restaurants. There are a few places hikers can find decently priced refuge, but many of those are toward the north of the city, farther away from the park. I had not been to Gatlinburg or Cherokee since my childhood.

While we were standing next to the road debating on whether or not to leave, a shuttle van stopped to drop off a group of thru-hikers heading north. As they disembarked, the driver shouted out to us. "You guys coming?"

"Nah, man, we're not going into town. Thanks, though!"

The thought was mighty tempting. If we had more time, a rest day in Gatlinburg would have been a nice way to break up the monotony of the mountains. The comforts of a night in a hotel would have gone a long way toward repairing my broken body and demoralized spirit. At that exact moment, each of us likely internally debated the pros and cons of quitting the trail. Perhaps we could come back to the park each day after waking up in a posh hotel, complete with room service and hot tubs. We could have seen the best the park had to offer from a car or hiked just a few short miles to any number of waterfalls or trails that we desired.

But we were resolute. Our dedication and probably our individual and combined stubbornness meant that we would finish what we started, regardless of what temptations we met along the way.

The three of us crossed the road and began to head up the hill toward the Mt. Collins shelter. The snow had begun to melt away at Newfound Gap, but as we continued to climb, the cold air brought down another light round. I was amazed at the difference between elevations. Just one thousand feet could mean ten or more degrees in temperature variation.

Shortly after passing over Newfound Gap, when we stopped to eat and rest in a small parking lot by the Clingman's Dome access road, a park ranger drove by. I was laying down on the grass against my pack soaking up the sun and resting my feet while the cars drove back and forth to Clingman's Dome. The sun had melted the snow on the hill and the warmth on our faces was most welcome.

"He's coming for you," Chris said as I sat up to see the ranger driving up to us.

This was the first time we had seen or spoken to a ranger in the park since we had arrived. Rangers were a rarity on the trail, which was both good and bad. I appreciated the freedom and wild nature of the trail. Rangers, regardless of their intentions, represented authority, but on the trail, the only authorities were nature itself and my own motivation.

The ranger drove a Ford SUV, fully decked out in National Park green and white. He rolled down the window and yelled over to us.

"Are you guys waiting for the shuttle to Gatlinburg?" he asked. The traditional spot for hiker shuttles was back at Newfound Gap. Perhaps he thought we were lost.

"No sir," I responded. "We're just taking a little break before heading down to Mt. Collins. We're going south on the trail."

Jeremy, still somewhat bitter about the lack of tarps covering the shelter at Icewater Springs the night before, asked the ranger why the park had taken down the tarps on some of the shelters ahead of a snowstorm.
"The winter season is pretty much over," he said. "It can get really hot and muggy inside of the shelters if we don't take down the tarps each spring."

"It didn't feel like spring with the snow we had," Jeremy said.

"I know, it's hard to predict the weather around this time of year. Well, you guys have a good hike and stay safe!" And with that, the ranger drove away.

"I like rangers way more than I like cops," Jeremy joked as the green and white SUV drove down the mountain road. I had thought of asking the ranger if he had a gallon of water I could borrow for a few moments, but I had no energy for banter.

By this point in the hike, I had grown tired of drinking water through my Sawyer Water Filter. I wanted to chug a gallon of water and was still disappointed that the water fountain at Newfound Gap was out of order. Sucking water through a tube was not very satisfying.

"It's good that the rangers at least know our plans and where we are," I told Jeremy and Chris.

Before we left, I had put together a list of all the shelters where we would be staying and on which nights. If there was an emergency back home, I imagined someone, somewhere would be able to get in contact with a ranger or ridge runner and leave a note for me in the shelter logbooks.

Each shelter has a spiral-bound, wide rule notebook inside where hikers would note their progress, leave notes for friends or simply offer a doodle or two. These were fascinating accounts of life on the trail but were obviously more relevant to those thru-hiking. Often, groups would stay together for a few days at a time, but become separated for whatever reason. Friendships developed and hikers found camaraderie in familiar people. Keeping track of lost friends and fellow hikers meant writing in and reading from the books left at each shelter. Often, we would see hikers reading the passages and notes, only to suddenly realize they were a day or two behind one of their friends and laugh or smile to themselves.

Chris, our newly designated guide, examined the map before we continued on from our break, pushing back up the mountain. For the first time in several days, we experienced the return of stairs. It seemed like areas closer to where tourists and day hikers might go featured plenty of stairs and switchbacks. Other, more remote areas of the trail we had seen, featured more rocks and roots than stairs away from all the parking lots and park entrances. Stairs were the enemy. I hated the stairs.

I stopped briefly next to a tree that had fallen alongside the trail. It was covered in snow. On it, I inscribed "Fuck Stairs." I was hopeful that someone, anyone, would see this and find a moment of humor in an otherwise cold and deadly serious place. The trail began to level off slightly and even featured a few switchbacks which allowed us to cruise at a decent pace for the first time since the morning.

The hike to Mt. Collins eventually flattened out altogether as we made our way through a densely wooded section. The walk through the woods bored Jeremy to tears, but I found the quiet white backdrop and subtle snowfall soothing. I had never hiked in the snow for this length of time before, and I was enjoying every minute of it. My boots held up well, despite the frozen slush below my feet.

The roots and rocks under the trail were difficult to spot as we marched through the cold. Several times in the flatter section, I kicked a rock or stump that would have broken my foot had it not been for my boots. The more I hiked, the more impressed I became with my footwear.

***

In the afternoon, we came to a unique section of the trail, a sectioned off portion of the park that had metal fencing running over several acres of forest. This section was created to help keep wild boar away from some of the park's endangered flora.

The trail here stepped up onto an elevated metal platform and cut back down the decline. All around the gate was barbed wire fencing. This section of trail seemed out of place set against the backdrop of otherwise pristine mountain hiking. For days, we had walked the ridgelines and under the treetops, never seeing man's undue influence outside of the shelters or the parking lot at Newfound Gap. But here, this metal monstrosity sat in stark contrast against the lush, living forest. It was painfully out of place.

Of all the animals that call the Great Smoky Mountain National Park home, the wild boar is among the most detested. The pig, originally from Europe, arrived in the late 19th century to the American southeast and thrived once it was able to escape into the wild. Wild boars are notorious for digging through and destroying vegetation, polluting the water supplies and spreading infectious diseases to other animals that live in the park. Because of this, boars are regularly hunted and hikers are asked to report any sighting to rangers or at visitor centers. Fortunately, we never saw a wild boar, but we saw plenty of signs of their presence throughout the park.

After passing through the protected area, we came to a section with several creek crossings that had been created from the snow runoff. Here, two or three smaller trees were lying over the water, offering a small, volunteer-made bushcraft bridge. These were terrifying and crossed over a dozen or more creek and watery sections along the path. As with the rain, the melting snow turned the trail into a runoff for the water as it rolled off the hills down into the valleys.

As we approached one of the bridges, my left foot slipped off to the side and my leg crashed into the freezing creek below. I came away mostly unscathed, no broken bones or sprains at least, but the remainder of the day, a dull pain shot through my left leg whenever I took a step. The others were more fortunate than I was, as they had stayed dry and kept their wits about them on the wintery obstacles.

By this point in the hike, all three of us had done something terrible to our bodies. Jeremy's knees were both bothering him, Chris had developed a few blisters on his feet and my left hip had suffered a surprise jolt and stubbing with each step toward the shelter. Still, we pushed on.

Finding water was not an issue in the park when the rain or snow fell. As the afternoon heat and sun began to melt away the top layers of snow, the trail turned back into the constantly flowing creek we had experienced the first few days. Mud, flowing water, slush and ice were constantly under our feet. The danger here was complacency. Twisting an ankle or hyperextending a knee could have been the end of the hike. While we were keen to make good time each day, none of us wanted to sacrifice speed for safety. I had already hurt myself that day and refused to seriously injure myself.

Eventually, we made it to the junction leading to the shelter. Mt. Collins was located about half a mile up the Sugarland Mountain Trail, off the Appalachian Trail north of Clingman's Dome. As we set off past the junction, the trail became a ditch, with high muddy walls and a mushy, slushy middle. This was a difficult section of trail to complete at the end of our day.

I tried carefully walking through the mess in an effort to keep my feet warm and dry, but it was no use. No matter how hard I tried to stay out of the mess on the trail, the path of least resistance often ran directly through the muck. My body hurt too badly to expend any additional effort. I wasn't worried about staying clean, but I had hoped to keep my pant legs and socks as dry as possible through the snow. It was pointless.

"Fuck it," I mumbled just loud enough for the other two to hear. "I'm just going to walk through it." I plowed through the brown snow slush, forgoing any attempt to keep my boots or lower pants dry.

Jeremy and Chris were hopping from side to side of the ditch to keep their feet warm and dry. Both were wearing trail runners, which didn't offer as much protection from the wetness as my boots, but were lighter and easier on the knees than my clunky mostly waterproof boots.

The half mile to the shelter flew by in just a few minutes. I was the first to arrive at Mt. Collins shelter because Jeremy and Chris had taken the section slowly. The slush and snow continued melting away, as I surveyed the surrounding area of the shelter.

Mt. Collins had a tarp over the sleeping area, a welcome addition to the previous night at Icebox. More importantly, we had beaten John Boy and Billy Bob to the shelter. The three of us gave a subdued, exhausted cheer for our victory over the other southbound hikers.

It was unusual for us to be the first to arrive at a shelter, but because we had only hiked six miles that day, the time on the trail was much shorter than our previous days. It also helped that a large section of the trail had been mostly flat and easy to navigate, even in the snow.

Chris was determined to start a fire to stave off the eventual chill, and the three of us unpacked before scavenging for burnable wood. Hiking kept the cold at bay, but when we arrived at the shelters, the stillness invited the freezing wind and chills.

Chris put music on his phone, the volume loud enough to wake a hibernating bear, while Jeremy and I got to work walking around the shelter. Tom Petty, Pearl Jam and other classic rock staples filled the cold air inside the shelter.

Fallen limbs, downed trees and other fuel was difficult to come by in and around the shelter. The effort was made doubly difficult by the fact that the snow and previous days' rains had soaked anything that might be otherwise burnable.

Previous hikers had cleared out most of the easily accessible wood long before we arrived that day. If we had ventured a half mile or more up or down the trail, we probably could have found a good deal of fallen limbs or sticks, but we scrounged where we could and grabbed whatever we thought might actually burn.

All around the shelter, fresh limbs had been cut or pulled from many of the trees. Almost all of the trees were alive and well and the branches cut or pulled off from many of them would be too green to even burn. This was a trend I noticed at several shelters, especially during the colder nights while looking for wood. It was disappointing to see such disrespect for the natural world around us.

I eventually found a downed tree and kicked off several of the limbs that were not touching the ground. That tree and nearly all the others that had fallen around the shelter were almost completely rotten or soaked through to the once mighty core thanks to the days of rain and snow. Picking up the sticks and broken off bits of the fallen trees stung our hands with bitter cold.

We somehow managed to find enough wood to make a small fire with the charcloth that I brought and a dab of Vaseline. We dubbed Chris the Twisted Firestarter after he got the fire going.

I'm a firestarter, twisted firestarter.
You're the firestarter, twisted firestarter.
I'm a firestarter, twisted firestarter starter.

***

A short while later, Minister Gem arrived at the shelter. She was in her mid-forties, chipper but visibly tired. Her spirits were high as she said she had completed her longest day yet on the trail, more than fifteen miles, she told us. Beginning her hike at Springer Mountain in Georgia, she had taken just over twenty days to make it to this portion of the trail in the Smokies.

Minister Gem was a religious outreach coordinator with a homeless advocacy organization in the Boston area. It had been her dream to hike the Appalachian Trail nearly her entire life, and she had recently taken a five-month sabbatical to complete as much of the trail as she could during her time away from work.

We later learned that she was married and planned to meet her husband several times along the way. Though she was unsure that she would make the entire trail in one attempt, she was pleased with her progress thus far and was more than willing to share whatever she could.

We apologized in advance for our crude language, but Minister Gem seemed carefree and even added her own mix of choice words more than a few times. She was the first minister I had ever heard say, "fuck." We quickly became friendly.

The four of us took turns drying our socks and boots by the fire. Each of us also had a hand in fanning the flames and stacking the wood in and around the fireplace. Minister Gem sat by the fire longer than the three of us. She had also walked further than the three of us.

We placed smaller pieces of wood inside of the fireplace near the fire in an effort to dry them. Once those became dry enough to burn, we dumped those into the fire and stacked more wood alongside the edge. This went on for what seemed like hours.

As we ate dinner, we talked about the past few days and mentioned to Minister Gem that she absolutely had to see Charlies Bunion. "It's the best part of the park north of here," I told her.

"Nope," she stubbornly responded. "I can't do that."

"But why?" I asked. "It's a tenth of a mile and it loops right back to the trail. It's really easy."

"I have to follow the markers," Minister Gem said. "I just zone out and follow the signs. I can't really help it, but I'm so determined to make it that I don't want to deviate from the trail at all."

"But ... you can just go back to the trail, you don't have to take the loop and skip anything. It's the coolest part of the park."

Minister Gem was adamant that she would not deviate from her hike, regardless of what incredible sites she would miss. The three of us found this ridiculous. I wondered what else she missed along the trail for fear of deviating from the path.

After dinner, the snow on the roof of the shelter began to give way. At first, the slow drop of clumps of snow came, but eventually, the entire roof's contents were dumped in front of the shelter in one glorious slide. Anyone standing under the roof in the wrong spot would have been buried up to their waist by the falling snow. I sat on the bench under the covered roof next to the falling snow. Jeremy and Chris were both outside, as well. As the snow began to fall, I let out a continuous moan of fake fear.

The combination of the short day and the light crowd made for an enjoyable evening. We continued to listen to music, ate and conversed while setting up our sleeping areas.

A short while later, another thru-hiker joined us at the shelter. He was visibly exhausted. Steam emanated from his back, his pack and the top of his head when he sat down inside. None of us had ever seen anything quite like it. He quickly ate, changed and crawled into his sleeping bag without saying much to the four of us.

Minister Gem, a hammock camper, was unable to find suitable trees near the shelter to set up her rig. She had no sleeping pad, as she had spent most of her nights sleeping in a hammock, but the outside cold and several feet of snow still collected on the ground necessitated her need to sleep inside. She hung up her rig on the top bunk to the far right and tried to make her bed as comfortable as possible given her circumstances. It must have been very difficult for her to find any comfort on the wooden bunk without any sort of meaningful padding.

"Some of the people I work with gave me an emergency blanket with a nice little note on it," she told us. "I'm going to use it tonight."

Despite the unusual setup, Minister Gem seemed to be pretty pleased with her sleeping arrangements as she crawled into her makeshift bed. Her hammock zipped up around her, providing a sort of cocoon of protection from the wind and bugs.

Minister Gem and I slept on the top bunk inside of the shelter. We discussed politics, my daughter, hiking and our hometowns. She was surprisingly liberal for someone who worked with a religious organization.

That night, after the five of us had all laid down, we saw a flash of light and heard several youthful voices call out into the darkness from outside the shelter.

"Hello!" one said.

"What's the password?" Jeremy yelled back.

"Cold. Cold mountain," the voice cracked in response.

Three teenage boys had wandered through the snow and ice in the darkness to arrive at the shelter in what must have been the most unprepared group of wilderness adventurers to ever tackle the Smokies. One of the boys was carrying a brand-new, never opened tent and none of the others had any sort of visible gear.

"What's the weather like here?" one of the boys asked somewhat timidly after marching through the plainly obvious snow.

"Well, it's cold and there's snow everywhere," Jeremy responded with a smirk. "Do you guys have any gear?"

"Not really," the kid holding the tent replied. He was wearing blue jeans and Chuck Taylors tennis shoes. One of the kids was wearing a t-shirt. How he and his friends made it to the shelter baffled us. "We were just going to set up a tent and camp."

"You don't have any sleeping bags or blankets?" I asked.

"No, do you think we need them?"

"Yeah, it's probably not a very good idea to sleep out here without some kind of gear. There's plenty of space in the bunks, though."

The three paused for a moment before finally admitting defeat. The trio had parked their car just a mile or so up the trail and had hiked in just before dusk.

"Let's just go back to the car," one said to his friends. And with that, the three said their goodbyes and headed back up the trail in the cold darkness.

Once the kids had left, everyone in the shelter burst into a raucous laughter.

"They had a brand new tent from K-Mart," Jeremy somehow made out through the laughter. "It's never even been unpacked."

"It was a Coleman with a 'K'," I quipped, somewhat proud of my quick wit.

Minister Gem found the encounter particularly hilarious. Her laughter was contagious.

"They probably just had some pot or booze or something and wanted to come party in the woods," Jeremy said.

The five of us giggled like school children until we fell asleep in the still cold.

Day Six
Riding the Ridge

THE SNOW WAS ALL BUT GONE when we woke up at Mt. Collins shelter. Ordinarily, we'd be on the trail around nine in the morning. Some days, we would linger a bit at the shelter if we had a shorter distance to traverse. On this morning, we decided we'd get off to a late start and ease into the day since we had plenty of time to make it to the next shelter at Double Spring Gap. The three of us collectively decided that spending more time on the trail and less time sitting in the shelters, waiting for the night to come, was the way to go. The last two days had been more difficult because of the cold and snow, but the sun's warmth and the prospect of epic mountain views were not to be taken for granted.

Even though I enjoyed the rest that came with relaxing at the shelters, it was too easy to get bored. Once we had set up our sleeping arrangements, ate and socialized with our temporary roommates, there was very little to do. The exciting parts of the trip, to us, were the views, the potential for animal encounters and seeing all the park had to offer.

At just over six miles, we had a strenuous, but manageable day ahead of us. Our hike would take us over Clingman's Dome, at sixty-six hundred feet above sea level, the highest point in the Great Smoky Mountains National Park and the highest point along the Appalachian Trail itself, to Double Spring Gap Shelter.

After walking further north on the Sugarland Mountain Trail to collect our water for the day, we made our way back up toward the Appalachian Trail, nearly a half mile to the south. After running into Minister Gem at the trail intersection, we said our final goodbyes and parted ways as she fiddled with her hiking poles.

All three of us were sad to see her go. It would have been easy to dismiss Minister Gem as annoyingly positive and upbeat, but her determination and humor were a refreshing change of pace from many of the other hikers we had encountered.. She had quickly become one of our favorites along the trail.

"I actually liked her," Jeremy said as we set off.

"Me too," Chris responded. "She was hilarious."

Our day was to begin with a short two-mile hike uphill to Clingman's Dome, followed by a few miles of mostly downhill portions to the shelter. After our earlier days on the trail, this seemed like a gift from the hiking gods. Mt. Collins was just over six thousand feet in elevation, and despite the elevation gain to the high point, the climb to Clingman's was not particularly steep, according to Chris' map reading and Minister Gem's recollection.

The snow had become a distant memory and by mid-morning, only a few patches in the shadows remained. It was remarkable that so much snow could fall and disappear in just two days' time. The fact that it was still early May and there had been snow on the ground at all still baffled us.

Jeremy, having somehow received a brief moment of phone reception at some point during the previous few days, had received a text message from his wife, complaining that it had been forty-seven degrees back home in Atlanta. She obviously had no idea what we were dealing with that week.

Even though the trails had again become a fairly consistent flow of runoff water, the sky was blue and mostly cloudless as we made our way up the mountains. For the first time in several days, we were able to walk free from snow or rain.

By this point in the hike, Jeremy and Chris were suffering almost as much as me. Their bodies were sore, just like mine, and nagging past injuries and lingering pain were in full force.

"My Hillary and my Trump are both shot," Jeremy told us on the way up to Clingman's Dome.

"Your Hillary and Trump?"

"Yeah, my knees," he responded. "They're both bad."

Our hike took place during the height of the 2016 presidential primary season. While we were in the woods, self-proclaimed real estate mogul and television personality Donald Trump had seemingly won the Republican primary process after his last two remaining rivals both dropped out of contention. We heard the news at Pecks Corner a few days earlier but avoided as much political bashing as possible when we were around other hikers. No matter how far away we were from normal, civilized society, political sensibilities could still be easily offended.

The three of us kept climbing toward the highest point of the park.

***

Around two hours into the day, Clingman's Dome came into view from the trail. We spotted the large concrete tower situated on top of the mountain. From where we stood, the tower appeared as a small structure on top of a very large hill. The more we walked up the ridgeline toward the mountain, the larger the tower became.

As we approached, we heard the faint sound of a small engine above us. Eventually, a small airplane flew past, caught an updraft, and turned to fly in the direction it had come after making a steep banking turn. The plane did this a few more times, each time becoming more aggressive about the glide and coast back toward the opposite direction. It was like our own little airshow, six thousand feet above sea level. We stopped to marvel at the plane each time it passed overhead.

The views coming up to Clingman's Dome were fantastic. The ridgeline began to open up slightly, and every so often, large boulders or rocks cut into the tree line, opening the views to the valley below.

We climbed along the top of the ridges until we came to a short stretch of downhill until the Clingman's Dome trail leading up to the mountain's summit. As we made our way further up the trail, the massive concrete tower atop the mountain came into full view. A short side trail took us up to the landmark tower.

We were again met with a sea of tourists.

The tower at Clingman's Dome climbed more than forty-five feet into the air. To access the observatory, a large walkway spiraled up to the tower's top. Snow and ice were still present on the walkway shadows, and watching the tourists climb up while trying not to slip and fall on the ice was comical, at least until I attempted to walk up and almost fell twice, as well.

There are three things in the world that I have always found particularly frightening: wasps, brain aneurysms and heights. Even so, I decided to walk to the top of the tower along with Jeremy and Chris and all of the tourists.

"I'm getting outside of my comfort zone!" I told the pair as I made my way up the tower's walkway clinging to the handrails.

Thanks to the tower, the park's tourists are given a picturesque three hundred and sixty-degree view of the surrounding mountains and valleys. A concrete bench circling the center of the tower was also particularly welcome and I spent most of my time sitting safely in the middle while Jeremy and Chris walked around the circular observation deck, taking photos.

The view was astonishing. There must have been a million trees all along the mountaintops and valleys below.

According to the U.S. Department of the Interior, there are more than one hundred different varieties of trees and at least a similar number of shrubs in the Great Smoky Mountains National Park.

Pine, oak, spruce, birch and poplar trees are some of the more common types of trees we continuously walked beneath during our hike. Despite the snow in the middle of the week, the spring leaves had already begun to color the canopy by the time we arrived and the bright greens and yellows gave us a sense of warmth in an otherwise frigid environment. As I had walked, I wished I had known more about the trees all around me.

Downed trees are everywhere along the trail. Due to the constant moisture and saturation of the rain, the ground had often become too soft to hold the weight of many of the giant trunks. This was a constant feature of the forests we encountered. It was uncommon to walk more than a few feet without noticing a downed tree somewhere alongside the path, particularly in the lower elevations where the ground was softer and the forests denser. To the credit of the park and its volunteers on the trail, very few, if any, downed trees actually blocked the trail, and those that did were quickly cut away to allow for easy foot travel.

The Fraser fir trees that dotted the highest elevations of the park had become sparse in recent years thanks to the balsam woolly adelgid, a small insect native to Europe that embeds itself into the firs and starves them of nutrients. Park officials claim that has much as eighty percent of the Fraser firs that once called the Great Smoky Mountains' highest elevations home have been destroyed since the insect first arrived at the Smokies just a few short decades ago.

While speaking with a volunteer at the base of the Clingman's Dome tower, I learned about the Fraser firs and the plight of the trees against the dreaded balsam woolly adelgid. I asked if acid rain was to blame.

"Pollution definitely doesn't help," the man told me. "The real problem, though, is the bugs."

"How does the park contain them?" I asked, genuinely curious.

"There's not a lot you can do. We just let them do their thing and hope that Frasers will develop some kind of natural defense against them," he continued. He then pointed to several smaller, perfectly healthy Fraser firs. "You see all of those young trees? They've all grown up since the insects have been here, so there's hope that they're developing a way to fight the bugs."

Only a few dozen young Fraser firs were set against the backdrop of an otherwise tattered landscape, but it was comforting to see that nature often finds a way to balance itself.

We disembarked from Clingman's Dome, and I decided that I needed bottled water since we were so close to the visitor's center below. About a half-mile down the hill from Clingman's Dome was a small store that sold chocolate, bottled water, stickers, t-shirts and stuffed animals. This diversion was completely necessary. I was dying.

Jeremy and Chris stayed by the tower while I walked the half mile down the hill to resupply and drop off my trash. This time, my bag was not nearly as full, but I wanted to toss it nonetheless. I offered to take Jeremy and Chris' trash, but they both refused. They did not refuse, however, the offer of chocolates.

After slowly making my way back up the hill with four bottles of water, six chocolate bars and twenty fewer dollars in my wallet, we prepared to set off again.

Before we marched down the mountain toward the shelter, I was able to find a brief moment of cell phone service. I quickly typed out a short text message to my parents and sister telling them I was okay.

"Hey! I made it to Clingman's Dome and have a signal. I'm fine! I'll see y'all in a few days," my message read.

The hike down Clingman's Dome was beautiful. For the first time all week, the skies were completely clear and cloudless. Ridge after ridge opened up to provide epic views of the surrounding mountains and hills. More than once, we stopped to soak in the glory of the mountains on a mountaintop meadow. Jeremy stopped often to take photos.

Wild blackberry bushes lined the ridges for miles. It was no wonder why so many bears inhabit this area of the country, I thought to myself. The bushes were bare, but I easily imagined a hilltop covered in wild blackberries.

This section was our reward. Finally. The views, the cool breeze and the shining sun washed away our cares. For a few moments, we had left the never-ending hike and had entered a warm and sunny hilltop paradise straight from The Sound of Music. Instead of the cold rain and snow we experienced just a day or two earlier, we were now walking with spring.

We came to a wreckage site where an old plane had smashed into the mountain many years prior. The crash was only a few feet from the trail, and Chris went off-trail to investigate. "There's not much there," he told us as he came back up the path. "I can't even tell if it was a plane."

A short while later, we heard two familiar voices on the trail coming up behind us. It was John Boy and Billy Bob. John Boy greeted us with excitement.

"Did y'all go to Gear Fest in Gatlinburg?" Billy Bob asked as the pair passed us on the trail.

"Beer Fest?" Jeremy misheard. "There's a beer festival in Gatlinburg? Shit, let's turn around now!"

"Oh no, gear fest, like hiking stuff." All three of us were incredibly disappointed.

John Boy and Billy Bob had gone to Gatlinburg the previous day instead of heading to Mt. Collins shelter where we had stayed the last night. Now we knew why they had not shown up as promised.

"We just had too much weight," John Boy told us. "We mailed a bunch of stuff to Fontana Dam to cut back. Plus, it was nice to get off the trail for the night and sleep in a bed." The pair had been on the trail just two days before stopping off in Gatlinburg to take a rest day.

"Oh, no wonder we didn't see you guys at the shelter last night. How much did you mail?" I asked.

"About ten pounds each," John Boy responded. "Most of that was food."

I was envious. A break from the hike would have been welcome, but I knew that starting back would be close to impossible after the last few days. Plus, we had no extra time. If our pace had been better or if we had requested more time off from work, we might have been able to justify a day in Gatlinburg. Still, the thought of not hiking for a day resonated with me.

John Boy and Billy Bob continued down the trail at a quick pace. Jeremy, Chris and I continued on, as well, albeit a bit slower to allow them time to get ahead of us. After the pair were far enough ahead of us to be out of earshot, Jeremy asked the obvious question.

"So, if there was a beer festival, we'd be going, right?"

"Uh, obviously," Chris responded. The sentiment was universal. At that moment, all three of us would have dropped our packs and left them in the middle of the trail for beer, a bed and a shower. But, there was no beer festival, and the hope of resting in Gatlinburg was dashed by the miles still ahead of us.

I had made a habit of apologizing at the end of each day for my attitude and general bitchiness. The nonexistent possibility of a beer festival weighed on my mind for the rest of the day's hike.

"I'm sorry for complaining, guys," I told Jeremy and Chris as we approached the shelter. "It's just my way of coping with how difficult this all is. I don't mean to bring anyone down. I'm having a good time, but I just struggled a lot today." I struggled a lot every day.

After bitching for hours during the uphill sections, I knew my attempt at self-penance largely fell on deaf ears. Still, it made me feel a little better to express some regret for my complaining, especially when Jeremy and Chris were not nearly as audibly frustrated as I had been during the day. If the roles had been reversed, I don't know if I would have been as calm and understanding as the brothers had been with me so far that week. Jeremy, in particular, was more supportive and understanding than he should have been.

**

We arrived at Double Spring shelter in the mid-afternoon, having taken more than a handful of lengthy breaks throughout the day. The trail cut right in front of the shelter, less than ten feet away, and the building sat on top of a ridge with a gorgeous overlook to the east. As we walked out of the woods toward the shelter, the scenery was reminiscent of what might appear in a Hansel and Gretel movie adaptation, maybe minus the candy cottage and creepy old lady looking to eat children.

There were a few hikers at the shelter already, including one named Moonshine. Two others were already eating and drying out their wet gear. The best part of each day had been arriving at the shelter, taking off our packs and realizing that we had no more miles to hike that day.

"How'd you get your trail name?" Chris asked Moonshine after a few pleasant introductions and a bit of unpacking.

"On one of our first days, I had a mason jar with moonshine in it, and we were giving it hikers as they came by a big rock where we were sitting. We got shit bombed that day. It made for a fun hike!"

Moonshine was a younger hiker, though probably not among the youngest we saw on the trail that week. He was about my height, maybe five foot ten inches tall, and had a short buzzed haircut. He had a sense of maturity about him that many of the other younger thru-hikers lacked. He was obviously not from privilege. The other two hikers at the shelter were a bit more reserved and quiet than our new friend.

Moonshine had an exterior framed Jansport backpack, an oddity on the trail. Most hikers we encountered had relatively new packs with futuristic ergonomic support systems, padded straps, air-flow mesh backing and other comfort features. Moonshine's pack looked like something that my father would have taken on a Boy Scout backpacking trip in the early seventies.

"I'm taking it back to the eighties on this hike," Moonshine told us proudly.

In truth, he later revealed, he purchased the pack because it was large and relatively inexpensive compared to many of the newer options commonly found on the trail. Whatever the reason, it was nice to see someone on the trail keeping the experience old fashioned even while I was struggling with more modern gear.

Earlier that day, we heard of a closure at Russell Field shelter further south because a bear had snuck in during the middle of the night and swiped an unsuspecting hiker's backpack from beside his tent. The hiker initially thought that someone had stolen his pack, but after a short search, his pack was found a few hundred yards away from the shelter in the woods tattered and destroyed. As it turned out, a bear had taken it during the night in search of food. Rangers decided the risk to potential hikers was too great and closed the shelter altogether. The rangers also set up a motion tracking camera to spot the bear should it return, we were told.

The hiker whose backpack was mauled by a bear was a friend of Moonshine's, and heading to our shelter that night. His pace that day, and every day was very slow, according to Moonshine.

"I can relate," I told him.

Between stories, I went off in search of the privy for the first time in several days. My bowels were heavy and ached as though I had eaten wet cement for the last week.

In addition to the shelter structure itself, most of the shelter areas in the park also had a small, purpose built privy for hiker use. These structures featured four three-quarter walls, a plastic toilet and a few buckets of mulch. As disgusting as they may sound, the privies were surprisingly clean, comfortable and not-at-all smelly. Most hikers respected them enough to treat them with care, something everyone on the trail appreciated.

Dropping a handful of mulch into the shit-collecting basket below both reduced the stench commonly associated with, well, human waste, and worked to break down and decompose whatever else was thrown into the privy, like toilet paper.

Signs lined the inside walls of the privy, reminding users just how to care for and utilize the facilities. Each privy was also wheelchair accessible, despite the park's trails being completely unable to reasonably accommodate anyone in a wheelchair. I found this bit of governmental regulation hilarious.

Jeremy and Chris had both been fairly regular on the trip, and by that point, had shit in the woods. I was lucky. I saved my bowel movements for the privy and had no accidents or other illness as a result.

After cleaning myself off and returning to the shelter, it was time to eat. We made our meals and gave away the leftover food from the day to anyone who would take it. Moonshine was more than happy to accept my mixed nuts and peanut butter for the day, and I was more than happy to ditch the weight.

Chris and Moonshine sat around the unused fire ring and talked about snowboarding for a while. The pair hit it off and shared stories about Colorado, California and even boarding in the Alps.

After eating, I hung up my food bags and noticed a tent set up behind the shelter.

"Are one of you guys set up behind the shelter?" I asked the group.

"No," one of the other hikers responded. "There are two girls set up back there, I think."

Girls! I was disappointed they weren't sleeping in the shelter with us, but that's probably why they were sleeping outside. Overly eager male hikers with bad jokes and musty ball sacks are likely the last thing most female hikers would want to encounter in the woods. I would imagine some women would actually prefer bear encounters to some of the encounters they had with male hikers.

We crawled into our sleeping bags and attempted to run out the clock on the remainder of the daylight.

I stayed awake later than normal that night playing a game on my phone as the sun faded behind the shelter. My portable battery charger began to fail earlier in the week from the cold, but I was able to get about seventy-five percent battery from it before it finally kicked the bucket. It was time to use the battery.

Chris brought with him a much larger portable charger, capable of charging his phone nearly a dozen times before it ran out of juice. Jeremy brought several smaller chargers and was able to keep a relatively powered phone battery for much of the hike, thanks to the variety of batteries he had on hand. So much so, that he could watch movies in his tent and in the shelters each night without fear of his phone completing dying as a result.

Despite having little to no cell phone service, we were still able to listen to music, play mindless games on our phones, watch movies or take notes about the trip with ease. Even in the vast remote wilderness we now called home, escaping technology was impossible. In our daily lives, these gadgets provide a constant connection to our friends, family and entertainment. As much as I tried to avoid my dependence on my phone during our hike, I still found myself wanting to listen to music at night.

That night, I thought of Horace Kephart and his adventures in the mountains more than one hundred years earlier. In his time, hiking and camping were very different than our experience in the woods today. I had ultra-lightweight aluminum trekking poles, Gor-Tex boots, water resistant fabrics covering my entire body, an ergonomic backpack and dehydrated meals for days. Kephart had a hand-carved wooden hiking stick, unsupportive leather boots, cotton clothing and rucksack. He had to forage or hunt for his food with the rifle he would carry with him.

I couldn't help but compare my struggle to his own. I wondered what Kephart would have thought of my fatigue and suffering despite my technological advances. He probably would have told me to man up. He probably would have shot me the first time I opened my mouth to complain about an uphill section. He probably would have questioned my fortitude and told me I had no place in the wilderness. He probably would have left me to die while he went off to hunt deer or some small game. In Kephart's world, he would have been right.

I fell asleep that night wishing I could live as Horace Kephart once lived.

***

"Hey Moonshine," an older man called out into the shelter long after dark as I fantasized about a simpler and more rugged time. The sound of his voice stirred me, and I sat up. "Come out and talk to me for a second."

Moonshine, who was already comfortably in his sleeping bag on the bottom bunk, got up, put on his shoes and walked outside of the shelter. I turned over on my stomach to see who was making all this commotion.

"And bring out the stove," the old man added. Ah, it was Moonshine's friend! Moonshine went into his pack and pulled out his cook kit.

The pair sat outside for a few minutes talking about the day's hike, though I could barely hear the conversation. The older man made pretty poor time, I heard, but he had some good news for Moonshine.

"I got us a crisp twenty dollar bill," he said. "We can go into Gatlinburg if you want." The muffled conversation faded in and out. Moonshine seemed too tired to care and came back inside without showing any excitement.

Eventually, the older hiker packed up his bag and hung his food from the bear lines hanging behind the shelter. After saying goodnight to Moonshine, he crawled into the bunk next to me and laid down. He was asleep within minutes.

I put in my earplugs and closed my eyes.

Day Seven
Nameless and Fearless

MY DREAMS ON THE TRAIL were vivid and intense. I dreamed about old girlfriends and past regrets. I dreamed about the Honda that I had recently traded in for a new (to me) Jeep. I dreamed about coworkers and the mass of emails that would be waiting for me when I returned to work. Even out in the woods, I was unable to escape the realities of my life.

Though the nights were rough, uncomfortable and cold, there was little to do at the shelters but rest. Hiker midnight happens sometime around sundown. Most nights, we were curled up in our sleeping bags, reading, listening to music or playing games on our phones long before hiker midnight. When darkness fell, it was easy to simply close your eyes and drift off to sleep. The exhaustion helped. Most of the hikers we encountered stuck to this schedule, though there were a few that would stay up late in their tents outside the shelter or would sleep until nearly everyone had gone in the morning. Our schedule fell somewhere in the middle.

In the morning, we met the two girls who had camped behind the shelter the night before. They were visibly shaken, and one appeared as though she had spent the better part of the night crying.

"There was a bear messing with our tent," one of the two said as we were eating breakfast. They were both gorgeous, one blonde, the other brunette, and both were tall and thin. It didn't take long before we were joking about the missed opportunity to play hero for the night and rescue the two beautiful women hiding away from the vicious bear.

It may have been the setting or the fact that the vast majority of hikers we saw were men, but whenever a beautiful woman came along the trail, one of us would claim her as our own, even as we marched on in the opposite direction knowing full well we would never see her again. Rarely did we see a woman hiking alone. More often than not, women on the trail were accompanying their presumed boyfriends or husbands.

Jeremy may have been happily married, but Chris and I were both struggling through the trail as single guys, without the prospect of a caring and loving wife to return home to once the hike ended. This meant we were particularly jovial and chipper whenever we came across a woman. No matter how grungy, disgusting or exhausted I felt at the time, I always had a smile for a pretty girl.

The girls were adamant they heard a bear. All of us questioned whether or not there actually had been one.

"Why didn't they scream or make any noise?" I wondered out loud. "There was a whole shelter of dudes here that would have jumped at the opportunity to help."

"I was probably the bear," Chris said.

"I bet it was the deer poking around in the field," Jeremy added.

All around the shelter that morning, a small group of deer walked around the grassy flat area munching on whatever it is deer eat. They had no fear of humans in the park, likely because no one had ever tried to shoot, attack or otherwise kill one of them. Though they were skittish at the sound of the wind and whenever anyone moved too closely, the deer mostly moseyed to and from outside of the shelter without a real care.

***

The Double Spring shelter was named because, naturally, it had two water springs. The first was on the North Carolina side of the state line and the second was on the Tennessee side. The views here were astounding. Several of the previous shelters had been nestled comfortably amongst the trees, but here, the shelter overlooked a steady decline down to the valley below. In the distance, four or five separate sets of ridges were clearly visible. This had been my favorite shelter so far.

Throughout the park, the Appalachian Trail largely hugs the state line between North Carolina and Tennessee. During our hike, we had straddled the state line for miles at a time, often crossing back and forth between the states a dozen times over only a few miles.

Our journey that day would take us from Double Spring shelter to Derrick Knob shelter, a total distance of around seven and a half miles. Packing up that morning was a breeze. The three of us had become extremely efficient at packing our gear, and only having two or three days' worth of food left meant that our packs were significantly lighter than when we had left Standing Bear a week earlier. Less weight and more space in our packs meant easier hiking for us. After saying our goodbyes to the damsels in distress and the few guys remaining at the shelter, we set off again.

For long stretches of time, we would walk in simple silence. Despite just meeting Chris a few days earlier, we had spent enough time together in the last few days to understand one another fairly well. While we had spent the early days talking feverishly about any and everything, we were, by now, comfortable with the silence.

When we did actually talk, we spoke about past adventures, women, life goals and, of course, what we would eat once the trip was over. It never took long for the topic of conversation to move to food. It was a pretty constant topic of conversation between the long periods of silence and my occasional moans about the never-ending inclines.

We talked about our favorite restaurants, our death row meals, our favorite individual foods and what we could eat for every single meal until we died.

The variety of food we had came in the form of the dehydrated meals we had brought. Chili mac, lasagna, macaroni and cheese, beef stroganoff, beef stew and a few other selections offered the only real choice of a meal on the trail. These were surprisingly good considering each had a shelf life of over more than a decade. Maybe it was the immense hunger or maybe the quality of these meals wasn't actually that bad, but we were all pleasantly surprised by the flavors. The only meals that were suspect were the breakfast packages that contained eggs. The eggs never rehydrated well enough to enjoy.

Unfortunately, I never quite mastered the ounce to milliliter conversion and often found myself drinking some version of stew instead of the meal. On the colder nights, this was actually a benefit, as they hydrated and warmed my body at the same time. As we neared the end of the hike and the temperatures began to climb again, the soupy messes became more difficult to enjoy.

Our hike for that day was about seven and a half miles, mostly downhill. Early in the day, we came to Silers Bald shelter, one of the first shelters we were able to actually skip in favor of one further down the trail. This, in itself, was a morale boost. We were back on our intended schedule and cruising. We stopped at the shelter, which was just off the trail, to resupply our water, snack and rest for a moment. We arrived slightly ahead of a large group, possibly a family, and not a single one of the hikers looked pleased with their progress for the day. If we were visibly exhausted, they were utterly miserable. We collected and filtered our water, ate quickly and moved on to the next destination without too much conversation.

***

The hike to the next shelter was mostly uneventful with a handful of stops and snack breaks. Only a few hours after leaving Double Spring, we arrived at the Derrick Knob shelter. We had made a good time that day thanks to the downhill portions and reduced weight on our backs. Despite this, we had hoped to spend a little more time on the trail and less time lounging around the shelter.

Scribbled on one of the benches under the covered roof of the shelter were the words "Chipmunk Palace." Beside the marking, a small arrow pointing to the inscription said simply, "No Joke!" All around the shelter, fat, furry chipmunks ran back and forth scavenging food scraps and making quite a racket. There were holes throughout the hills and flat land next to the shelter, which made picking a tent spot particularly challenging for Jeremy and Chris.

Sitting outside of the shelter was a long-haired man we later learned was called Nameless. There was also a lesbian couple lounging in the sun, filtering water into their water bottles. Both were planning on hiking up to Silers Bald later in the day.

Nameless had a dog with him, which he called Fearless, so named because his dog scared away the bears without any hesitation. Fearless looked malnourished. Her ribs stood out against her body and she seemed to have very little energy for anything other than laying down in the dirt by the shelter and collecting flies. How this dog was able to hike as regularly and far as her owner was surprising to me. I offered to give her food in the form of a meat stick, but Nameless refused the offer.

"She gets really bad gas when she eats people food," Nameless explained, "and I have to sleep with her!"

Nameless told us of his travels around the country by train, his failed past attempts on the trail and how he enjoyed night hiking without a headlamp better than hiking during the day.

"Especially when the full moon is out," he said.

Nameless was a traveler and likely had no home or family, outside of his dog Fearless.

He had been at Derrick Knob since the previous night's hike. It was late afternoon now, and he was eating and prepping for another late afternoon departure. He walked around the shelter in a pair of Japanese wooden sandals as he gathered his gear. He was unlike any hiker we had met on the trail thus far. He lacked a seriousness about completing the trail and seemed to be hiking just to have something to do with his life.

Nameless smoked spliff cigarettes. He never offered one to me, which was a bit disappointing after I had given him more than half of my day's food allotment in the form of mixed nuts and peanut butter. I would have seriously enjoyed one.

"This is my second year on the trail," he told us. "Last year my shoes gave out in Nantahala. I hiked three days without any shoes and had to give up. When I got to the forest, all the people there looked at me like I was crazy!"

Nantahala National Forest sits just south of the Great Smoky Mountains National Park and is a shorter and a slightly easier section of the Appalachian Trail than the section we were attempting.

Briefly, I wondered why Nameless didn't simply buy a new pair of shoes but then realized his transient nature answered the question for me. He very likely could not have afforded a new pair of shoes. The kindness of strangers must not have extended to new boots for the trail.

After a while, the lesbian couple decided to head out for the next shelter north, and a short while after, Nameless and Fearless also left.

Later that afternoon, a crowd began to arrive at the shelter. There was a nice mix of young and old that night, including a few old timers that were more than happy to share their experiences on the trail with anyone that would listen. The diverse crowd was a pleasant experience.

I went off in search of water. Nearly all of the shelters we had come across had water sources relatively close to them. In most cases, water was only a few feet away from the shelter or trail. In others, it was further away, like Derrick Knob shelter, where it was down a rather lengthy hill with two switchbacks and several large boulders to traverse.

Most of the water sources were pipes pushed deep into the ground near a spring. The water would flow, cold and clear, from the metal pipes. When there had been a substantial rain, the water flowed more freely. Sometimes, though, the water would only come in a steady trickle.

After returning to the shelter with four liters of water, I sat near the fire and ate as the sun began to fall behind the shelter.

Coming up the hill, toward the shelter from the south, was a giant of a man. Standing at 7'1" and clocking in at over three hundred pounds, he struggled to make it up the final hill to the shelter, leaning against his thick wooden walking stick.

The man, called The Bear, was well known to some of the thru-hikers. That day had been his longest day on the trail so far, some fourteen miles. It was late, already near dusk when he arrived, and after making it to a soft, grassy patch near the shelter, he collapsed onto the ground, breathing as if he had just run a hundred consecutive marathons.

I had never seen someone so large attempt something as difficult as a thru-hike of the trail. His body was massive and he was visibly drained. After several moments, he collected himself and began to set up his tent, collect water and hang his food. Everyone in our group was bemused by The Bear's size and just how much energy it must take on a daily basis for this man to complete the sections of trail ahead of him.

Jeremy was a little too loud in commenting on The Bear's size, but the gentle giant either didn't hear or was otherwise unfazed by the comments on his size. He had probably heard it all before.

After finishing his tasks, The Bear ate and joked with everyone at the shelter about his hike. He and another thru-hiker, a woman called Hop-A-Long, discussed their days, the views from the ridgeline and asked about mutual friends who were ahead or behind them on the trail. Both read through the shelter log.

"I leaned against a tree today to rest," The Bear told her. "I accidentally pushed it over." Everyone laughed.

Because of the immense amount of rain that falls in the Smokies every year, downed trees are fairly common. Several times during our trip newly fallen trees had blocked part or all of the trail. While the trail volunteers and park staff do an incredible job of keeping everything as tidy as possible, there are just too many fallen trees to tackle to ensure a perfectly clear path all of the time. This was expected, but to hear The Bear tell his story, it sounded as though the tree he pushed over may not have been completely dead.

Another man at the shelter that night was a section hiker going north. He had no trail name, but he did have an interesting story. The former Navy pilot flew missions tracking Russian and Chinese submarines over the Pacific Ocean. His job, he said, was to be ready to destroy Russian subs before they could fire their nuclear missiles.

Another hiker at the shelter that night was an older woman, probably the oldest person that we had seen on the trail thus far. She arrived after us, with a pack that must have weighed as much as she did, but her enthusiasm for adventure was contagious. She wore a hat with patches sewn on, some much newer than others, featuring locations of her previous hikes. She wasn't going to Maine, but she was as rugged and prepared as anyone we met along the way.

It was difficult to keep my questions to myself. I asked about her family and husband, her history in the mountains, her gear and attitude. She explained that she began hiking decades ago, but that her husband never really cared for it. Her family enjoyed the wilderness, she said, as long as they were in a cabin or RV.

She gave me several Aleve, which by that point in the hike was like manna to my aching legs and feet. I ate the entire handful at once and prayed for quick release.

Chris built a fire and a few of us walked around the shelter area to gather wood, which was again sparse near the structure. The fire made enough smoke to keep the bugs away, probably Chris' goal, and some of us gathered around the fire pit to share stories and talk about our trail experiences while eating our dehydrated meals.

Shortly before dark, two younger hikers arrived at the shelter. As the two put together their tents and prepared food, one of the hikers opened his backpack and pulled out a large Ziploc bag filled with smaller Ziploc bags all containing various pills and medicines.

"Caffeine, sleeping pills, Aleve, Tylenol, uppers, downers, energy pills," he explained to another one of the thru-hikers. "I heard that the body's histamines block the first six hundred milligrams of whatever you take," he added. "So you gotta take a lot of whatever it is you need!"

For a moment, the poor kid's eyes appeared as though they would bulge out of their sockets. He kept mumbling about wanting to play. Play what? I wasn't sure. It was pretty clear to me that he had eaten enough medication since starting the trail to clean out an entire pharmacy.

That night, for the first time since leaving Standing Bear Farms, I was able to use my hammock. I had learned a valuable lesson from my first attempt and instead of trying to tie knots to hold my tarp and hammock in place, I used the hardware I had purchased beforehand, which worked like a charm.

I had spent a good deal of time ahead of the hike watching YouTube videos and reading how-to guides to learn a variety of knots. The one knot I did end up using on my guidelines was the Prusik knot, a sort of friction loop knot that tightened when the line is pulled and allows for sliding up and down the guideline when the tension is released. The other knots I learned did not work the way I had imagined or prepared. Perhaps I hadn't learned as much as I thought.

I was worried about using a hammock in the park because, as I saw it, bears see things that hang from trees as food. My biggest goal was to avoid being swiped or bitten in the middle of the night by a hungry, giant ball of fur with teeth. With the number of people at the shelter that night and my penchant for snoring loud enough to wake the dead, I wasn't too worried, but I kept the thought in the back of my mind nonetheless.

Before setting off, I had read about an incident in 2015 where a father and son were hammock camping in the southern Smokies. The son was dragged out of his hammock in the middle of the night and attacked by a bear, but survived mostly unscathed. It's possible that the son may have had some kind of food on his person, but bears have learned that bags equal food, and a hammock looks an awful lot like a bag filled with human meat when it's suspended between two trees.

I was extra careful that night to remove everything from my clothes that could possibly attract a bear. As I drifted off, there was no energy left for worry. The soft, suspending hammock felt like a cloud under my back. I had the most comfortable and restful night of sleep that I had had in more than a week.

Why hadn't I used the hammock more often?

Day Eight
Pissing on Rocky Top

AS I STIRRED IN MY HAMMOCK that morning, I reflected on how far we had come. With only twenty or so miles left in the hike, the realization that we had come nearly sixty miles began to set in.

Our hike today would take us from Derrick Knob shelter to Mollies Ridge shelter, the last shelter we would stay at during our trip and the first shelter northbound thru-hikers come to when entering the Smokies. The trail would take us some twelve miles over Thunderhead Mountain and Rocky Top. It was going to be a long day.

I packed away my hammock gear and traded breakfast with Jeremy. Chocolate covered Pop Tarts were a welcome treat after starting each of my previous mornings with a protein Nature Valley and Cliff bars. Jeremy felt the same.

"I fucking hate Pop Tarts," he kept saying. He seemed relieved. In truth, I was, as well. My daily allotment of Cliff bars had become a bland and unexciting way to begin each morning. Jeremy joked that the chocolate fudge bar looked and tasted like a flattened turd. He was right.

I walked to the water supply and filled my large hydration bags with more than two liters, while Jeremy and Chris took off to shit. When

I came back, I squeezed the water through my filter into the plastic bottles I had picked up from the gift shop at Clingman's Dome.

After we had eaten and packed away our gear, we set off for two of the park's most famous mountains.

***

I've had years of cramped up city life
Trapped like a duck in a pen
Now all I know is it's a pity life
Can't be simple again.

Rocky Top you'll always be
Home sweet home to me
Good ol' Rocky Top
Rocky Top Tennessee, Rocky Top Tennessee

Rocky Top, written by Felice and Boudleaux Bryant and popularized by the Osborne Brothers in 1967, is unofficially the official song of the University of Tennessee. As a southern boy, raised in Bulldog country and representing the University of Georgia, I was particularly thrilled to tackle one of Tennessee's most famous natural landmarks. I planned to leave my mark.

"I'm going to take a shit on it," I told Jeremy and Chris, only half joking, on the slow hike up the mountain.

Thru-hikers have a different sense of connection to their surroundings on the trail than section hikers or day hikers. To a thru-hiker, every mountain is an obstacle, a hunk of dirt and rock that must be climbed and descended. Some hunks of dirt and rock are taller, steeper and tougher than others, but they're essentially all the same. Section hikers have more of an opportunity to appreciate their

120

surroundings, the views and the overall experience because they're on the trail to experience just that singular part.

We asked several of the hikers that we passed that morning if we were approaching Rocky Top. Not a single one of them knew the name of the mountain, whether or not they had crossed it, or if we were anywhere close.

"There was one back there that had a lot of rocks on it," one thru-hiker told us. "So, maybe?"

The name of the mountains didn't seem to matter to many of the thru-hikers we had met along the trail. The individual experiences and views didn't really matter to many of them either. The only thing that was important was how far they had gone that day and how far they had left to go before they could eat and sleep. Thru-hikers have a way of compartmentalizing the day, taking the hike as it comes and moving on to the next hike without much fanfare. There were only two monumental milestones along the Appalachian Trail, the beginning at Springer Mountain and the end at Katahdin. Everything between was nothing more than a sideshow for the bookends.

Why even bother hiking a trail if you're not going to pay attention to what's on it?

**

That morning we came upon Mt. Davis, one of the worst individual climbs since the first day. Though not particularly tall compared to some of the park's higher peaks, the five thousand foot Mt. Davis was a complete and total bitch. We climbed hundreds of feet in a relatively short distance, over large boulders and massive roots. Each little climb was ten or more feet, and each of these sections burned our bodies and drained our will to hike further. We stopped many times on the incline to rest and to catch our breath. Even Jeremy and Chris were thankful for my many stops.

I pushed up the mountain, struggling to progress with each step. After an intense, but short climb, we made it to the top of the mountain to see a small plaque stuck to a rock at the summit.

Each of us gave our collective "fuck you" to the mountain. We had another battle cry that would last until well after the hike: fuck Mt. Davis!

We made our way down to the next ridge and onto Thunderhead Mountain, which sat just a few hundred yards away from Rocky Top. Both mountains were massive and filled the sky as we approached. The trail here climbed hundreds of feet. We knew it would take a while to reach the summit at our average pace. Most of the mountains we climbed appeared grossly massive from a distance, but, as we neared, seemed to appear more manageable. Thunderhead did not. Even as we approached, its immense size never scaled down.

On our way toward the base of the mountain, I heard a rustling in the woods and a quick black flash crossed the trail and continued off down the hill. It was another black bear, but this time, it was more interested in running away from us than what we might be carrying in our packs. The three of us watched briefly as the bear hustled off into the brush. Our second bear encounter had been much more pleasant than our first.

When we stopped for a moment to rest at the base of the mountain, I scratched the bridge of my nose. I felt the immediate sensation I'd come to dread: a pop followed by an immediate nosebleed. Throughout the snow days, spots of blood would drip down onto my beard from my nose, but these were easy enough to wipe away. Those were nothing compared to what I was now experiencing.

For the better part of my life, an ill-timed scratch or walking into a particularly dry or humid room would cause a fountain of blood to pour from my right nostril. I had grown accustomed to this over the years, and even kept a pack of tissues in my desk at work for such an occasion. But out here in the woods, there was no bathroom for me to run to and tidy up. There was no sink to wash my face after. There was no emergency room to drive to in case I simply could not stop bleeding. Out here, bleeding to death, even from the nose, was wholly possible.

It was gross.

Jeremy, excited at the prospect of playing EMT, pulled out his first aid kit. I held a handkerchief against my nose, pressing it against my face with as much force as I could muster. We sat along the rocks beside the trail as two hikers heading north passed by.

"Oh, look, there's blood on the trail," one of them told the other.

"Eww!"

After more than half an hour of waiting trailside, I cut off a few pieces of gauze and stuffed them up my nostrils. I put a few extra pieces in my shirt pocket, in case I needed backup.

I continued up the hill, gauze and all. A few hikers that we passed made jokes, but a few were sympathetic to my crippling condition.

Eventually, we reached Thunderhead Mountain. We climbed a few of the boulders and large rocks on the summit to get a better view and it was spectacular. A plate monument attached to a large rock at the top of the ridgeline announced the mountain's height: 5,528 feet.

After a short uphill, we made it to the summit. Here, there was another small plaque showing the elevation. Why hadn't all the mountains in the park featured these plaques?

Thunderhead featured several large boulders and a few amazing scenic overlooks poking out above the foliage. We stopped to check out the views, and I made sure to check and recheck the gauze. So far, so good.

Rocky Top was just a few hundred feet from Thunderhead, and we pushed on toward what was said to be the best view in the entire park.

We came to a clearing with another plaque and more large boulders. This was it! Rocky Top. I walked right over to the largest, closest boulder I could find, pulled down my shorts and pissed all over the rock. Unfortunately, we had not quite made it to the top. I had wasted my piss!

We continued up to the actual summit, where Jeremy did the deed for the three of us. Earlier in the day, I had entertained the idea of taking a shit on the mountain but there was nothing there to push through. I settled for Jeremy's piss while having a good laugh.

We marveled at the sight. There were only a handful of mountains in the park that were visibly taller. The mountains and valleys below filled the view. This is why we suffered, literally bled and walked mile after mile with broken bodies and sapped spirits. This view was without a doubt the best of the entire park.

I sat down on one of the many rocks and removed the gauze from my nose. By this point, it had been an hour or so since I had spit out blood from my sinuses. Again, so far so good. I cleaned myself off as best I could, while I heard Jeremy and Chris laughing from above.

"It looks like a lot of people have pissed up here," Jeremy said.

The hike down the ridgeline from Rocky Top took us down more than five hundred feet in elevation. There were several flat, grassy fields that were perfect for a rest. We stopped several times to relax, eat and soak up the warm sun. For the first time, we were able to hike in relative comfort without the need for rain, snow or wind protection. I was wearing my shin-high socks, shorts and a short sleeve microfiber shirt.

A while later, we crossed Spence Field and moved onto to Russell Field. Russell Field, where Moonshine's friend had had his backpack stolen by a bear two nights earlier, was still closed while rangers were attempting to locate and track the furry culprit. The bear, if caught, would likely be euthanized.

As we approached Russell Field shelter, we saw, for the first time, an announcement of a shelter closing nailed to one of the overhang posts. There was also a tracking camera attached to a tree a few dozen feet away from the shelter, pointing back toward the main structure. I posed in front of the camera for a few action shots.

The shelter here was situated in the middle of a flattened section of forest and probably would have been one of my favorites had we had stayed there. While we read the sign, a female hiker approached from the south and joined us to investigate the shelter closing for herself.

We chatted briefly about the shelter and the bears. It was her second day in the park, and she was anxious to push ahead as quickly as possible. We said our goodbyes, wished her luck and continued toward Mollies Ridge.

The last half of the day coming down from Rocky Top was very light. Thanks to the flat and largely downhill portions, we made a good time, despite the distance and rest breaks. Even with the easier terrain, our bodies still suffered.

For the first time since entering the Smokies, we had several miles of flat or nearly flat hiking. Chris and I promised to shower the mountains with gifts if the trail stayed flat for the remainder of the day.

***

The long distance hiking had done strange things to my body. My shoulders constantly ached. My hips felt as though I had carried a small elephant tied around my waist with a rope the entire trail. But perhaps the worst pain I experienced came from the chafing. Somehow, it was my ass that suffered the most. I had never experienced a problem with chafing before, but I had never attempted anything quite like this hike before. It only took a day or two before my body's constant rubbing against itself began to take a toll. By this point in the trip, my inner thighs, testicles and ass cheeks were all rubbed raw. This was something I had heard very little about before we began.

Jeremy and Chris had both brought Gold Bond powder with them. Chris had been kind enough to let me use some of his Gold Bond each morning before we set off from the shelter. His only rule was that I could not touch him with my right hand after I applied the powder. That was only fair. Despite the Gold Bond, the chafing continued

126

nearly every day and was, by far, the most physically uncomfortable aspect of my hike. Each morning, I rubbed Gold Bond on my ass crack, my balls, my feet and whatever else I felt needed protection that day. I was thankful Chris was willing to share.

When I had first begun seriously hiking a few years earlier, the boots I purchased were cheaply made and cheaply priced. Many of my initial physical issues from hiking were foot-related. In the months leading up to the hike, I purchased new hiking boots, the single most expensive pair of shoes I've ever bought. I wore them day hikes to break them in and became quite enamored with the quality and how well they performed under various conditions. Through the rain, snow and rocks, my boots held up incredibly well.

"When I get back home, I'm going to write a review of these boots," I told Jeremy and Chris. "They're my favorite piece of gear by far." Each afternoon when we arrived at a shelter, I would take off my boots and put on a pair of inexpensive flip-flops that I had picked up from Wal-Mart a few months earlier. These foam shoes served their purpose, allowing me to air out my feet after a long day, but in truth, my boots were much more comfortable.

Jeremy and Chris had identical trail runners in identical sizes. One pair had been made in India while the other was made in Vietnam. Chris eventually burned a small part of his shoe's sole to mark which pair belonged to him. Both had also brought along camp shoes.

I had expected my feet to give me the most problems on the trail. I brought moleskin with me for the anticipated blisters, but those never came. At this point in the hike, my feet were pristine at the end of the day, albeit a little pruned from the moisture. I believed this success was due to a combination of my boots and socks.

All of my socks were merino wool. Many hikers we met chose to hike in synthetic socks. I knew that if I were going to wear boots for nine days straight that I would want the thickest, best possible quality socks I could find. I had packed away four pairs: two ankle high, one shin high and one nearly knee high pair. The fourth pair, I thought while packing, would be a luxury, but all four pairs had become necessary after days of hiking in the rain and snow. Jeremy and I were both envious of Chris' seemingly never-ending supply of dry, warm and clean socks.

Our clothes were filthy, and we smelled like death. I had not showered in over a week, probably the longest period of time in my life that I had not seriously cleaned myself. My pants were caked in dried mud and my socks were nearly stiff. It would be a relief to finally shower and change into something clean.

***

We arrived at Mollies Ridge early in the evening and ran into two familiar faces, John Boy and Billy Bob. Both had hiked from Silers Bald shelter to Mollies Ridge earlier in the day. John Boy gave us a big smile as he high-fived each of us. It was their last night on the trail, as well. John Boy told us about their day while Billy Bob maintained the fire.

Mollies Ridge was full, and most of the hikers staying there that night were younger. Russell Field, just a few miles up the trail, was closed, and that meant more people were forced to stay at Mollies Ridge instead of pushing onto Silers Bald. The shelter closing had a ripple effect on the hiking bubbles. Instead of evening out the crowds, hikers had to decide if they would push on or play it safe. Most of the hikers we met played it safe.

Several of the thru-hikers were sitting around the fire as we took off our packs and set about getting ready for the night. The sun had faded behind the hills and the crowd around the fire was boisterous and loud. While boiling the water for our dehydrated meals, we discussed the day with John Boy. He was even more excited than the last time we had seen him.

"Dude! It's good to see you guys again," I told him. "How was your hike? Did you go over Rocky Top today?"

"Oh hell yeah, we went on Rocky Top. I'm from Mississippi, and I don't really care for Tennessee," John Boy said with a mischievous grin. "So, I took a piss up on Rocky Top."

"We did the same thing!" I told him. "Well, I wasted mine. I took a piss on the side of Rocky Top. Jeremy made it all the way to the summit."

This was hilarious to our group. We couldn't imagine how many people have had the same thought and done exactly what we did on the top of Tennessee's most famous mountain. How many Georgia, Alabama, Mississippi and North Carolina hikers had defaced a Tennessee landmark?

"I wanted to take a shit up there," I told him, "but I didn't have to go! I was pretty bummed." John Boy laughed.

He told us how they had run into an older man who was hiking with his son. The man, obviously drunk, was drinking cans of beer on top of the mountain and singing old country classics as John Boy and Billy Bob approached.

"He was drunk as fuck, it was hilarious. He was just pissing all over the place. He had his dick out and everything!"

"I wonder how many people have actually taken a piss on Rocky Top," Chris mused aloud. "I bet thousands."

That night, as I was cleaning out the last bit of food from my dry sack, I came across the pack of tortillas that I had stuffed in the bottom more than a week earlier. I pulled out the package, examined the nutritional value and noticed the weight. Sixteen ounces!

I had carried a pound of tortillas for eight days! A fucking useless, burdensome and unconsumed pound of bland tortillas. I joked about the added weight with one of the other hikers, but he had little sympathy for me.

"I can't believe this has been in my pack the entire week, and I haven't even touched it yet," I said. "A fucking pound!"

The hiker offered to help me eat as many as he could and a few moments later the tortillas were being passed around the camp. Many of the thru-hikers had resupplied before coming into the park. As we made our way toward our eventual end, it became more difficult to give away our extra food, but I had little trouble getting rid of the tortillas.

I decided to eat two dehydrated meals that night to knock out even more weight and space. Chili mac, a particular favorite, and lasagna were both on the menu tonight. I ate the lasagna with a handful of tortillas, soaking up the meat sauce as best I could.

Since we had arrived late to the shelter, most of the bunk space was had already been taken. A few thru-hikers volunteered to move out of the way for us, and we were able to set up our sleeping pads. I was situated on the top bunk wedged between two thru-hikers. Jeremy and Chris found spots on the bottom bunk.

That night, John Boy and Billy Bob stayed up to tend the fire and talk after everyone else had gone to sleep. I laid on my stomach and watched the embers from afar as I tried to drift off. There was not enough battery on my phone to listen to music or play any games. Tonight, my only entertainment was the fire.

Tomorrow would be our final day in the park, and tomorrow night I would be home again. A small part of me was excited to go home, shower, drink six beers and fall fast asleep in my own bed. Another part of me was already missing the trail and everything that came with it. We had come so far in the last seven days. There were a million reasons why I should want to be home at that very moment instead of wedged between two strangers on a wooden bunk in the middle of a forest, but none of those reasons mattered as I fell asleep that evening.

I was home, even if only for one more day.

Day Nine
There and Back Again

WE WOKE THAT MORNING at Mollies Ridge, full of anticipation for our final day on the trail. Time passes differently in the woods, and though we were sad to see the end the hike just a few hours away, our bodies and stomachs had suffered enough to make the prospect of a warm bed, fried chicken, wine and beer seem like Christmas morning. I had mixed feelings about leaving the park and wanted to enjoy as much of the forest as I could before returning to Atlanta.

There were still some eleven or twelve miles ahead of us, but the vast majority of these, particularly the last full section of the day, was completely downhill. My knees and ankles had held up well during the previous eight days, and I was confident that this would be my time to shine. No more slogging for me! I would be like the nimble and speedy mountain goat while my companions would be the ones suffering. That was the plan, at least.

We gathered water, prepared food for breakfast and set off from the shelter much earlier than normal. Our last day was a march down the mountains to Fontana Dam, where we had parked the van more than a week before. There were a few – three, according to Chris – smaller uphill portions early in the day, but these were only a few hundred feet high each.

The feeling was unreal. Despite the bruises, insect bites, soreness and general grumpiness I felt every morning after leaving the shelter, my body and mind were in good shape for our final day. We were determined to make a good time and had already begun making plans for our immediate post-hike meal. We decided on fried chicken.

"I can't wait to get home," Jeremy said. "I'm going to drink two bottles of wine."

"I'm going to take an hour-long shower, and then I'm going to take an hour-long bath," Chris added.

By this point in the trip, Chris had become extremely adept at reading the trail map. So much so, we had dubbed him Mapquest as his unofficial trail name. His readings were pretty spot on, much to our chagrin when he announced a series of uphill sections.

"We have three uphill sections before the downhill," he said. "I didn't want to say anything, but the first mountain is around six hundred feet."

The news was soul crushing. After reviewing someone's elevation chart a day earlier, I had been certain that the last day would be completely downhill, save for a few, easy flat portions. My dreams of a carefree walk were tempered as we set off that morning.

Still, the hike that day was easier than I had expected. Large portions of the trail were nearly flat. We begged the mountains to keep up the trend, and for several miles, the mountains obliged. At one point, we walked for perhaps three or four miles on nearly completely flat trail. We began to wonder why we had taken the reverse approach to our hike by coming south instead of north. The northbound hikers had a much easier trail to navigate.

There were no more shelters between us and the end of the park. The last remaining landmark was Shuckstack Fire Tower, and with our beds so close, none of us were even remotely interested in climbing the metal stairs for yet another mountaintop view.

We pushed on through flat, slightly uphill and downhill sections of the trail for several miles before nearing our midpoint for the day.

The bugs were out in full force. Hiking in the snow had spoiled us, as we had not had to deal with a substantial number of insects since the first morning when we had set off from Standing Bear Farms. For me, the problem was the endless swarms of gnats. My heavy breathing and constant sweaty head and face attracted more of the bugs than I could deal with. Finally, it felt like summer, for us and for the bugs.

The gnats constantly flew into my nose, my eyes and my ears. It made for a miserable hike. I counted no less than six gnats that had flown directly into my right eye. With each stinging sensation, I became more incensed. Eventually, my frustration got the better of me, and I pulled out a piece of gear that I had kept secret until now. It was a bug net. For my head. I made Jeremy and Chris promise not to make fun of me as I put it on.

The net protected my eyeball from the bugs, but my breathing still attracted them to the outside of the net. The gnats gathered on the netting and crawled around, inches away from my face. The bug-net worked, but it was very uncomfortable. The hot air pouring out of my mouth with each exhale warmed the net and kept the stale breaths close to my face. There was no winning today.

I noticed that the worst of the bugs came when we stopped to rest or when my pace slowed enough to allow the bugs the opportunity to catch up to my face. As long as I kept moving at a decent pace, the bugs would not have the chance to crash into my face and lay their eggs directly on my corneas. I kept this in mind as I continued and struggled to maintain a decent speed hiking uphill.

Jeremy and Chris were also suffering. Jeremy's knees had been bothering him for several days at this point, but today, his pace was the slowest it had been during the entire hike. Even with the reduced pack weight, the hike down the hills was intense.

"This is the hardest day so far," Jeremy told us. My legs were tired but held up well. It was odd being the hiker from our group in the best shape, after spending the previous week struggling at every turn.

The hike took us further and further down the mountains, from around forty-five hundred feet at Mollies Ridge to around eighteen hundred by the time we reached Fontana Dam.

Our final bear encounter came that afternoon. As we were walking along a mostly flat path, I heard a rustle in the bushes up the trail. Our group stopped and listened. We thought the bear had moved down the hill, away from the trail. We threw rocks down into the valley near a large group of bushes and trees where we guessed the bear had run to hide.

As we approached where we had heard the sounds, the rustling stopped, and we assumed the bear was gone.

I was in the front of the pack as I came to a tree on the right of the trail. As I passed the tree, I looked down and saw a black bear just a few feet away from me. It looked up at me from below as I let out the manliest shout I could muster. It was so close that I could have reached out and touched the bear with my hiking poles if I had felt like losing a limb.

"Whoa!" I shouted. The bear seemed unfazed by my intrusion, but it began to walk down the hill to the valley floor. It took all of my courage not to turn around and run back toward the others. I caught myself turning away, but the bear had no interest in attacking me or anyone in my group that afternoon.

Behind us were two-day hikers that had come to see Shuckstack. As they approached our position on the trail, Jeremy took out his camera and began to snap photos as the bear made its way downhill. The five of us stopped to watch the animal mosey its way out of sight into the brush.

When we arrived at the Shuckstack junction, the couple behind told us that another bear we had not noticed was also down in the valley, leaning against a fallen tree.

As disappointing as it would have been not to see a bear during the entire trip, I began to wonder if our luck had run out and the next encounter would not be as pleasant, considering the inherent danger of seeing and interacting with wild animals in their native habitats. Since we were on our way out of the park, seeing another bear was unlikely, though not impossible.

We later learned that on our last day in the park, a hiker had been attacked by a bear while in his tent. The hiker had been bitten on the leg. He survived, and a few days later, a bear believed to be behind the attack was captured and euthanized, but it was later revealed by DNA evidence that the bear killed was not the one actually responsible for the attack.

A handful of bears are euthanized every year in the park, mostly after becoming too familiar with hikers and campers. Bears that stick around shelters seeking an easy meal are tracked, tranquilized and sometimes killed in order to protect the fragile balance between man and nature.

***

As we approached a rock outcrop, a northbound thru-hiker stood thirty feet ahead of us, frozen in her tracks.

"Watch out, there's a rattlesnake up here," she shouted toward us.

We carefully approached and saw the snake ahead. It was a timber rattlesnake, nearly four feet in length, and it was pissed off. The trail fell off to the right, and to the left, a large rock face climbing some fifteen feet above us prevented any real way of climbing past the snake.

"I've been standing here, like thirty minutes, waiting for it to move," the hiker said. The snake was coiled in the middle of the trail, unimpressed with our need to get home.

Rattlesnakes are not intimidated by humans. While a bear or boar might scurry off when approached by a hiker, this creature knew that it could fuck up most anything it came across and did not act as though it was at all frightened.

Eventually, the rattlesnake slithered toward a small puddle on the rock, stuck its head in the water and stayed there for several moments. We waited for it to move, but it refused to even acknowledge us. Eventually, Jeremy tossed a rock at it, causing the snake to coil up again and rattle its tail furiously, ready to strike at whatever came within distance.

We spent the next ten or so minutes urging the snake to leave the trail, sometimes agitating it, sometimes just waiting impatiently. Eventually, it began crawling back toward the thru-hiker. She climbed up the rock face, threw her pack down to me and slid down until she made it beyond the snake unscathed.

She scurried off in search of a suitable lunch spot, while the three of us stood a few feet behind the snake waiting for enough space to run past.

Eventually, the snake made its way up the hill and down to the side of the trail. When it was far enough off the trail for us to feel safe, we each scurried past it, moving more quickly than we had the entire week. Chris ran first. Then it was my turn. My backpack flopped against my back as I ran by. Jeremy brought up the rear. Once we had safely made it past the snake, the three of us had a good laugh.

Shortly after we had moved beyond the snake, we shifted from the rock outcrop back into the forest.

The last stretch of intense downhill was around five miles. In this portion, our group descended nearly three thousand feet. While covering the distance was easy on the lungs, it began to take a toll on my legs, knees and ankles. Jeremy and Chris, who had made good times during the uphill portions earlier in the week, were now the ones suffering through fatigue and pain. My legs were tired, but for once, I was in the best shape.

During a particularly rough section of uphill, I had joked earlier in the week that my knees were the only good part of my body. My lungs, not at all helped by my pack a day smoking habit, could barely power me through the uphill sections. At least during the downhill portions, the biggest burden was on my legs.

Uphill hiking tested my cardio. Downhill hiking tested my strength. My heart and lungs may have been suspect during the trip, but at least my legs were up to the task of the constant drop. It was a tough walk, but not nearly as tough as the first two days of the hike had been.

My pace had improved slightly during the week. I wasn't sure if this was because my pack weighed almost twenty pounds lighter or if I had grown somewhat accustomed to the mountains. Maybe it was both.

The last downhill section seemed to go on and on. After making remarkably good time, at least for us, during the flatter and uphill sections that day, the last bit of downhill seemed never-ending. We took turns moaning and groaning about the last stretch of trail and how, again, the park's signs were merely an estimation of how far we had to actually travel. As with the previous days, the last mile through the park was unquestionably the longest.

To kill time, we began planning a similar trip, for the same time next year.

"Maybe we can do something a little less strenuous," Jeremy suggested. "Like, hike in and camp for a couple of days and move on."

"This definitely didn't feel like a vacation," Chris responded. "Maybe a working vacation."

"I'd love to be able to do a little fishing on the next trip," I chimed in.

We discussed several possible destinations: Banff National Park in Canada, Yosemite National Park in California, even a weeklong Iceland excursion. Since we had the appropriate gear, we thought we could spend the money next year on travel instead of supplies as we had done to prepare for this trip.

Finally, Fontana Lake came into view below us. As we continued down the trail, the lake became more even with our field of view, but it was still a slow, uneven descent. We were only a few hundred feet above the water, and the end was in sight with every step forward. Still, it seemed like we hiked for an hour or two after first spotting the water. Each of us assumed the end was around the next corner or down the next gap. But finally, the trees broke ahead of us on the trail, a large sign appeared and a paved road became clearly visible.

***

We made it to the end of the park without any real fanfare. We were exhausted, sore and smelled like death. I held my hiking poles meekly over my head as we crossed the park line and stopped briefly to read the signboard leading into the trail.

There were more warnings of bears and a map of the trail leading into the park going north. It had not dawned on me until much later that tens of thousands of hikers before me had probably stopped there, as well, dreading the coming hills and mountains we had just completed.

We had succeeded in our goal by going the opposite direction toward the south.

Our attention turned to the van, which was only a few short miles from the end of the park. After more than eighty miles of rock, gravel and dirt, the paved road under our feet hurt and stung my heels with each step. The ground was flat, and we held out hope that a passerby would feel bad for us and drive us to the other side of the dam.

The three of us decided to walk along the well-worn footpath next to the access road, instead of on the paved road. The dirt trail felt natural compared to the hard pavement, and our feet, swollen and battered from the day's steep decline, needed every last bit of cushioning they could get on that final stretch. The sun shined through the trees lining the road. It was hot, hotter than any day of the trip so far, and we made every effort to stay in the shade.

Through rain, sleet, snow, fog, green trees, bare trees and now the hot, shining sun, it felt like we had walked through all four of the seasons in nine days.

A few minutes after we had left the park, Fontana Dam came into view around the tree line. This sight of the dam was more impactful than the Great Smoky Mountains National Park Appalachian Trail boundary itself had been just moments earlier. We walked for a half mile more until we were on top of the dam, which, too, seemed to go on forever.

Fontana Dam was built as a part of the Tennessee Valley Authority construction projects during World War 2. Standing over four hundred and eighty feet high and nearly a half-mile in length, the dam is one of the highest dams in the eastern United States. We stepped back onto the road and turned toward the parking lot on the other side of the waterway, as the heat radiated from the pavement below.

Walking on top of the dam was terrifying. I stayed as far away from the railing as possible, without walking directly on the road. Slowly, but surely, we came ever closer to the van.

Spurred on by the prospect of finally finishing our goal, the three of us had made remarkable time that day. In a little more than seven hours, we had hiked nearly thirteen miles, by far our best mileage per hour of the hike. After beginning the day believing it would take ten or more hours to make it to the van, we were thrilled with our progress and continued on, encouraged by the morale boost.

"I really thought it would take all day," Chris said. "We killed it!"

As we approached the van, we reminisced about the adventure behind us. We had seen bears, deer, rabbits, snakes and turkeys. We had seen rock-covered mountaintops and lush, green valleys that were home to millions of trees. We had met dozens of hikers along the way that helped shape our experience on the trail, for better and for worse.

We had hiked more than eighty miles through lightning, snow and clear skies, and though we were all broken and exhausted, the hills and mountains were now behind us. Only the pavement, the road and our homes were ahead of us.

The collective mood was jovial. The sense of accomplishment was overwhelming, but we were too exhausted to properly celebrate. There were no photo ops, no poses or self-snapped photos. There was only walking.

Once we made it to the Fontana Dam parking lot, I spotted a mother and daughter getting ready to walk across the sun-drenched dam road. The mother was smoking a cigarette. I quickly hurried over and made fast friends by telling her about our hike, before asking if I could have one of her cigarettes.

"You hiked the whole park?" she asked, as she handed me a menthol cigarette.

"Yes ma'am," I responded. "You see that fire tower up on the mountain up there?" I pointed to the top of one of the nearby mountains to Shuckstack Tower.

"Sure do."

"That's where we came from today. All the way down the mountains to the dam here. It was about twelve or thirteen miles today."

"You hiked all that way in one day?" she asked.

I nodded in response. "I think our total was somewhere around eighty miles over the last eight days."

The woman fell silent before asking if she could take my photo. I feebly brushed my hair with my fingers in a failed attempt to make myself somewhat presentable for her camera. I must have looked a complete mess.

"As long as you promise to make me internet famous!" I told her.

She snapped my picture and departed for the far side of the dam a few moments later.

I returned to the van, my blood again pumping with nicotine, more content and exhausted than I had ever been. The three of us piled into the van, threw off our dirty shoes and boots and reveled in the van's air conditioning for several moments before speaking. There was a brief moment of reflection for each of us.

It would have been easy to regret the decision to hike the Appalachian Trail through the Smokies, and at times during the hike itself, I was full of doubt. It had been beyond demanding. My body and spirit had been tested, and though I may have touched failure more than once during the trip, I had made it to the end. I had conquered the mountains.

Earlier in the week, Jeremy had asked if I regretted the decision to hike the trail. I tried to respond with a positive answer but fell short when the words actually came out of my mouth. I paused a few seconds before I could answer him.

"I don't regret it," I told him. "But I've never done anything this physically demanding before. I'm getting my ass kicked constantly."

I would have given the same response if asked during our hike out, as well. I did not regret the hike, and now that we had completed the more than eighty miles, I was disappointed to leave. I knew once I was gone that I would miss the simplicity of being on the trail. Part of me wanted to turn around and walk north again.

Maybe I could catch up with Minister Gem, Nameless, Hop-a-Long, M&M or any number of the other thru-hikers we had met and walk all the way to Maine. I could spend the next four months hiking, ignoring life's responsibilities and living the ultimate adventure to completion. But, I couldn't. That's what made finishing the hike through the Smokies so bittersweet.

Throughout our eight days in the park, I didn't learn any life-changing lessons. I had no spiritual awakening nor developed any real connection to nature. My worldview was largely the same entering the park as leaving, but the experiences, both positive and negative, echoed in my mind as we drove away from the dam. Soon, the lake fell away behind the shoreline trees and hills.

The soreness and exhaustion were a very real and very present reminder of just how far we had come. The challenge had tested both my physical and mental fortitude.

This would forever be an adventure I'd remember, but now it was time to find some fried chicken, biscuits, gravy and anything other than water to drink.

.

Made in the USA
Lexington, KY
02 August 2018